YOU.....

CAN HOOK RUGS

by

PEARL K. McGOWN

Other Books by PEARL K. McGOWN
"The Dreams Beneath Design"

Library of Congress Catalog Card Number 53-7958
First Printing — May, 1951
Second Printing — April, 1953
Third Printing — November, 1959

This book is dedicated to my son, Winthrop H. McGown and my sisters, May Brooks, Sylvia Bartlett and Kaddy McCabe, without whom it might never have been written.

INDEX OF CONTENTS

LIST OF ILLUSTRATIONS

*Color

Rose Cottage

ROSE COTTAGE

The subject of hooked rugs is interwoven inextricably with the creation of Rose Cottage. Rose Cottage was a dream. It became reality! It is of this dream that I should like to tell you. Perhaps you have already visited Rose Cottage. You may be familiar with the story behind this home of hooked rugs, but since there are those who are not, let me here record it.

Rose Cottage is my gift to you, especially you who love to hook rugs. As the realization of my dream, it is a place where you may come to study hooked rugs and to gain inspiration for creative work. It is also my home, encompassing all that the word implies.

Although my hobby later grew into a business, I never lost my love of hooking, or my desire to be of service to those who desired to transform my designs into rugs of lasting beauty and loveliness.

It all started in 1930 in such a small way, when I made my first rug design. My interest grew and expanded as my designs increased in number. As the first ripple from a pebble thrown into a lake reaches out to distant shores, just so did my interest expand into the lives of many people. This craft is not limited to women. It is shared by men and children too!

During those earliest years, the immediate problem of finding time to pursue my hobby and to study all the fascinating things about it, left me no time to imagine what might later develop. In those years, I was filling first my own need for an interest, and in doing so, I was also fulfilling the need of a woman — any woman — just one at a time, who might want a certain type of rug designed especially for her home. I never thought of applying a true financial value to what I was doing. It did not occur to me that the small price received from the sale of a pattern did not repay me for a tenth of the time required to design it. I loved what I was doing! I was concerned only with fulfilling the desire of that particular woman. And so, in trying to satisfy the desires of many different individuals, I gradually accumulated a great many types of designs. Today I have more than a thousand.

There was little time in which to pursue my hobby, for since I was employed full time in a law office, there were only evenings in which to perform all the household duties necessary to maintain a home for my son. But like all those who have an absorbing hobby, I rode it every spare moment. When you really want to do something, you will find the time for doing it — if your desire is strong enough!

My progress was infinitely slow — too slow to realize that the diligence required to produce new patterns would eventually result in a pyramid. Those early years were full of obstacles! I had no training. It was thrilling to find I could do something of which I had never dreamed. I had no funds. My supplies had to be gathered the hard way. I had so little time. I was always torn between joy and duty, — the joy in designing and my duties as Mother and homemaker. Much of my designing had to be done after my son had retired for the night, for we had much to discuss about his school affairs. Many times, long after midnight, sister May (who lived in my lower apartment) would call to ask, "Are you going to work ALL night?"

There were challenges too, — and one was space. You have no idea how much truck you can gather when your hobby is hooked rugs. (Or have you?) Luckily, I had a large attic which became my workshop. But I needed shelf room mostly, and you can't build shelves on slanting walls. All straight walls were shelved and all closets filled with shelves, and still my stock of supplies grew larger. Ever since then I have had shelf trouble, building them in every conceivable place and piling them high until they shrieked with their loads. But there never were enough!

About this time I realized if I was really going to know what was "hookable" I must hook myself, and so more supplies accumulated. Now frames, bags, boxes, trunks filled with rags, — and mountains of scrap books began to pile up. I saved everything!

Filing drawers became necessary, for I had to be able to turn to what I wanted when I needed it most. Magazines were riddled and articles filed away under their proper headings. Soon the attic began to bulge. Then this bulge began to spread throughout the house. A small space in my kitchen made one more closet for more rags! A set of boxes just fitted under the kitchen table to hold more rags. Clothes closets were rearranged to provide more space for more boxes, and more rags.

During this period I had to also personally produce the patterns on burlap, and also keep my books of records. But since I was distributing all my designs at that time through only one teacher (Mrs. Caroline C. Saunders) of this craft, bookkeeping was quite simple. But as her classes grew, so did the demand for the patterns. I needed help! My first appeal was to my son, of high-school age, who helped me to reproduce the patterns on burlap. But he, too, had a hobby. He had an orchestra, (oh, ours was a busy life!), so soon some of his school friends were pressed into service. But football and basketball and other sports demanded their time. Finally sister May came to my rescue, and for a long time turned out all the patterns.

Those were busy days, and burning the candle at both ends made a pretty light, but brought about an enforced rest for one summer. My mind seethed with the stories which I had gathered about the designs I had copied or collected. It seemed a pity not to record them and pass them on to others. Thus my book "The Dreams Beneath Design"* was born, and kept my mind and fingers busy while I rested.

1938 was a year in which things began to happen. My book was published. My son was married, and naturally became involved in making a new way of life for himself. Competent pupils of the first teacher were now reaching out toward passing their ability on to others. They wanted to become teachers in

---

*A complete listing of all publications by Pearl K. McGown is to be found in the back of the book.

their own right. They came to my home to choose and discuss their patterns. So my bedroom was sacrificed for a Studio. My father-in-law, who had retired, was now glad to assist May in reproducing the patterns, to fill his idle time. May began to help the teachers in the Studio with their choice of patterns.

About this time I began to realize that dyed materials were very necessary to secure an artistic effect in a hooked rug. I interested my friend Hattie, who painted and had a flair for color, in dyeing swatches, so that in one grouping of colors you would find all the gradations of hue, or accents of color necessary to make a rose, a tulip or some other particular flower. But where could I keep these new swatches? Separating the different hues required space and more space. There was nothing to do but sacrifice my dressing room for a swatch room, so these walls too were lined with shelves reaching to the ceiling. They made a pretty sight!

Almost immediately another challenge presented itself. The correspondence through these years had increased tremendously. Even with clerical help, which called for dictation in the evening, it became a difficult problem with which to cope. All this kept me more and more from doing that which I loved most — my designing.

Sister May was having her "shelf trouble" too. There simply had to be more shelves to keep the patterns separated, so that she could find the patterns she was seeking without undue delay! She had "time trouble" too, for no matter how she adjusted and readjusted her meal periods, someone was sure to ring the bell just as she was about to sit down to eat! The tail was beginning to wag the dog!

By 1940 I began to realize that teachers were having problems too. They needed help, and since the revival of this craft was, so to speak, in its infancy, there were too few places for them to turn for help. I gave this teacher problem a great deal of thought and decided that by sharing their problems with each other it would be mutually beneficial. I could do my part too, in suggest-

ing and guiding and discussing. Discussion was the thing! Let
them bring their rugs to a group meeting and let us have a
friendly discussion about them. Why not an exhibit of finished
rugs? You can see how one thought led to another, and thus, the
Teachers' Annual Exhibit was born, with a full day to discuss
our common problems before the Exhibit was opened to the public. The first two were held at the historic Old Colonial Inn, in
Concord, Massachusetts, and the third one in the Copley Plaza
Hotel, in Boston. By 1943, because we were at war and the gaso-
line shortage made traveling practically impossible, we chose
Horticultural Hall, in Worcester, Massachusetts.

Here they have since become an anticipated pleasure to thousands of ruggers each May. Allen Eaton, in his book entitled
"Handicrafts of New England," says: "These exhibitions are
attended by persons from all parts of New England and from
many other states. The various processes of dyeing and hooking
are demonstrated. Prepared materials with instructions as to how
they may be used with some of the patterns, are available at
reasonable cost. There is a general interchange of ideas and experiences among hookers and teachers. This is probably the most
important annual gathering of rug makers in our country. With
its exhibitions, demonstrations, and general information, it is the
starting place for many workers in this popular folk art."

These teachers who now represent a good share of the states,
not only send in impressive examples of their best work each year,
but they travel from all over the country to attend our Teachers'
Conferences just previous to these Exhibits. For, in sponsoring
this craft, my main idea has been to give, give, give, — for only
as we give shall we receive. In the meantime, when war was
declared in December 1941, I realized that burlap would become a
strategic item and be unobtainable. Therefore, the activity of our
craft was threatened just at a time when women most needed this
outlet for their morale. And so, in order to sustain their courage
and to give impetus to their interest, I started a monthly publica-

tion called the LETTER SERVICE. It was in the nature of general instruction in the art of shading and highlighting some particular flower, leaf or detail of a design. But most of all, it was to include subjects of interest to ruggers which might hold our group together until this awful period of war was over.

By 1943 there was a request that all teachers and their most adept pupils volunteer their services in teaching this craft under the Arts & Skills program of the Red Cross in the Military Hospitals. The long, lonely and ofttimes painful hours spent by our boys might be eased, through various types of recreation, and hooking was to be taught as such. Every rugger was eager to do for some boy that which she would like some other mother to do for hers.

As "Headcraftsman" of this craft, I was assisted by 28 women four days a week in a program which kept an average of 140 boys hooking all the time. It was a bit difficult to interest the boys at first. Then I hit upon the idea of enlarging the insignia of their own outfits to a 15" or 18" size and they could hook it in its true colors. This subject had a meaning to them, and the pattern completed could be used as a wall hanging. Later they made bags, chair seats, footstools and rugs.

Woolen mills were most generous in sending us huge quantities for this purpose, the Bell Mfg. Co. of Worcester, Mass. being among the most frequent and generous of donors. The "shelf" space problem followed me here. Each craft or skill taught in the Hospital was allotted the smallest margin of space absolutely necessary for its supplies. So one of my greatest problems was that of securing adequate storage for materials donated. But the authorities were understanding and helpful, and our program was very successful.

Of course my designing was laid aside for the duration of the war. Every possible moment was devoted to enlarging more than 100 insignia for the boys or developing their own ideas into patterns. The Red Cross was instrumental in supplying us with burlap.

So many incidents stand out in my memory from that experience. One was the cleverness of one patient. He asked for a plain piece of burlap and said he was going to make a valentine for his wife. Asked if he had hooked before, he said: "No, but I think I can manage." At first we were skeptical, but after we had provided the various hues he asked for, we watched him take a snapshot from his pocket and sketch a few lines on the burlap from it. The first few loops he awkwardly pulled into the burlap, but he soon caught on. Then gradually we saw something happen to that burlap. A large heart was drawn to form a frame, and the area around it was hooked in red. Within, a face of delicate light tones began to take shape. Dark brown formed the hair. Dark shadows fell upon the neck. Deep blue eyes and subtly shaded lines gave character to the face. A fuchsia lower lip and an orangey upper lip made us gasp! But, lo and behold, when completed and hung upon the opposite wall, every detail was perfect, and the orange of the upper lip became a highlight. We later learned he was a most accomplished photographer. I don't think any sweetheart received a more unique valentine!

Hooking seemed quite natural to many of the boys, and you could never imagine how proud they were of their work. One of the boys made and carved a footstool and hooked a top for it. It was very well done. Not knowing the circumstances of the boy, and thinking to help him, I asked him if he would like to sell it. "Lady, are you crazy?" he said incredulously, "I wouldn't sell that footstool for $200."

Of course we had to sometimes coax them to hook, or to keep at it after they started, but there would always be some who eagerly awaited each lesson. One boy made a rug while lying flat upon his back. The frame was suspended over him just high enough so that he could reach the lower part. His technique was perfect! Every loop was pulled in evenly and with great precision.

Doctors, with hand injuries, who had themselves been helped through hooking, advised all patients with similar injuries to hook

to limber up their muscles. One of the teachers even taught a blind boy to hook! His facial injury was beyond description, so he was always alone and behind a screen. She hooked the outlines of a geometric square which formed a sort of hooked Braille. Then, from a medley of colors, which she placed in certain positions on his frame, he could choose the desired color. He had beautiful hands! When he left for Valley Forge for face surgery, he was much less lonely than he had been before he started handcraft.

How tired we used to get! We tramped what seemed like miles of ramps between wards. And at the end of the day there would be delays, waiting for busses and a long ride home. But it was worth it!

During this time women were begging me to stamp designs upon scraps of their own burlap, for they had found that hooking kept their minds off the tragedies of war. They sent me every type of burlap, even laundered grain bags. I also bought grain bags myself. We utilized coarse linen (many of the old rugs were hooked on homespun linen) and monk's cloth (when I could find it — though it was scarce as the proverbial "hen's teeth"). How we ever managed to keep everybody's grain bag separate and get it back to the right person is beyond me now, and of course occasionally we didn't. I would never repeat that experience again!

By 1945 and the end of the war, the craft took on a new impetus. Established teachers, gaining new inspiration from each annual Exhibit, were now showing increased progress, and each year new teachers were added to our group. This meant more visitors to my home, and since I was still employed at business full time, sister May was bearing the brunt of this increased activity.

About this time sister Sylvia (oh yes, I have six of them), who had retired from bank work, came to live with me. She is a perfectionist in office work and figures, and oh, the joy of shifting these duties to her capable hands! I shall never forget, though, her dismay at the apparent disorder of my desk when she took over. My correspondence had increased to the point where it was always piled high. Each pile had a particular meaning to me — some awaiting color plans — some needing information not readily attainable — requests for certain designs, memos and notes. To Sylvia it was just a mess! So she said: "Well the first thing I'm going to do is clean up your desk!" Thank heaven that in the pursuit of my hobby I had learned to keep a silent tongue at certain times when others did not quite understand my problems. Today I get a great chuckle when I occasionally rib her about the various piles of different problems which she accumulates on her desk. She has learned that banking and the hooking business are not at all alike!

In the meantime, the flower swatches were becoming increasingly popular. So more and more of them were made. Where to keep them? Shelves were full and now big boxes were being shoved into every conceivable corner, heaped in every closet, and stored even under my bed!

By this time I was taking one day off a week so I could have a teacher come to my home to conduct a class. I wanted to be closer to the ruggers' problems. It also enabled me to do more hooking myself, or to supervise rugs made for me by others, and to carry out certain other ideas. For these classes we hired May's rooms downstairs. So we were really bulging out all over. I was getting desperate! Oh, how I needed more room!

Now I began to spend hours studying the rear of my house — and trying to visualize how an addition might affect its appearance. My father had been a building contractor and many times I had drawn his plans. Would such an addition be large enough for a class room too? I toyed with ruler and pencil planning on paper, and in my mind I built a dozen or more additions until I had one that seemed just right. I then took the plans to a contractor and almost swooned when I heard the price of its construction. My dream practically vanished!

I have always been a great believer in: "Not my will, but Thine be done." I usually see the day when I can say: "Thank you, Lord, for your guidance!" Thus it was that one day as I was looking out my kitchen window, the yellow cottage across the field, which I had always loved, seemed actually to beckon to me! Its owner had recently died. As if by divine intent, I met the Executor face to face on the street next day. I asked: "What are you going to do with the cottage?" She replied: "Sell, I guess! You know, Pearl, there is an unusually large room over the kitchen that would make a priceless work room for someone." Right then and there my dream was again in the making! But like most dreams, it didn't just happen then. It took a pile of figuring. I had my strong days when I simply must have it and never tired of figuring ways it might be possible. I had my weak days when I gave it all up. There were so many obstacles — so many challenges — for this was during the years when building materials were practically non-existent!

Every confab with a heating or building contractor made the whole project seem more impossible. And then a little voice would say: "Nothing is impossible except as you make it so. Anything worthwhile is worth struggling for." That was when I had to have faith. I would talk to myself thus: "This thing I want is a place for ALL to enjoy — it is not a selfish desire. What I've earned I want to share with others. What I've learned I want to give to others." Then I would look at the lovely rugs which I had slowly accumulated, and think: "They would be such an inspiration to others!" Oh, to have an adequate place to which others might come to observe and learn! Surely this was a good desire and it would be blessed.

And so I drew and re-drew my plans of how the cottage might be adjusted to my dream, but the total sum always seemed to spell ruin to my plans. And so I finally resigned myself to giving it all up.

And then a strange thing happened. The Executor called me and said: "I will make a concession to you on price. I would rather you had the cottage than to sell it to one who might possibly turn it and the barn into several small apartments, for it is too near my own home for that." What better indication that my dream was meant to be? I returned to my pencil and figuring!

And what figuring! Have you ever restored a house? Then you know that no matter how you figure, it always costs more than you estimate. And added to that was the scarcity of materials, especially plumbing and heating equipment. After I had ordered them I spent almost every lunch hour hounding them by phone or camping on their doorstep, hoping they'd get so sick of seeing me that they'd give me the stuff to get rid of me. And I had to be SO adjustable! If I couldn't get what I asked for (and I usually couldn't), I must take what I could get, and usually at a higher price. When the extra bills came in my heart would sink, and then I'd say: "Well, if I can only find more women who want to hook or teach, perhaps I can make the grade. Keep faith!"

To make matters worse, I had a chance to sell my old house before my new one was ready. Now think of those shelves and their load which had to be moved but could not be set in place, for there was still much painting and papering going on at the cottage. Think of confining in the four available rooms all that was contained in seven rooms with their bulging shelves and closets. Now think of living in these confined quarters and conducting a business there too, for three months! You know, at moments like these, you keep your sanity by saying to yourself: "There is always an end to everything — this thing can't go on forever." And so it was, that gradually the paint pots were cleared away — we ceased to stumble over paperhanger's equipment and bump into electricians and plumbers — and the final pieces of the jigsaw puzzle slipped into place.

Out of this melee emerged a Studio where my hostess could

display patterns and other materials, two offices, a classroom, and an extremely large workshop for my designing. Best of all, some lovely old pine floors which were scraped, filled and waxed, were a perfect setting for my hooked rugs. A large, almost new barn was converted into a production and printing shop. This became such a busy place that we called it the "Bee Hive." (Some one heard me referring to the Hive one day and said: "Oh, do you keep bees too?") A rear ell, which had been a woodshed, was remodeled, and lo! a small apartment was provided for May and her husband. Sister Sylvia and I settled down to a normal life.

By this time my dream house took on a personality that demanded a name. And almost by way of an answer to this problem, one day the Executor said to me: "You know, Pearl, it was called Rose Cottage fifty years ago when my Uncle purchased the property." "ROSE"— no flower was more familiar to me, for it appeared in most of my designs. No name could be more appropriate, and so its original name — ROSE COTTAGE — was restored. Roses were planted so that in season there might be a bowl of them to greet you!

Since we live in the rooms you visit, we are obliged to confine your visiting hours to Monday through Friday (holidays excepted) from 1:45 to 5 P.M.

DO drop in!

And now you may wonder why I have told you about my struggle. I have told you these things because there are those who are tempted to give up their dreams against what seem insurmountable odds! But have faith! All good things can come to pass! Go on dreaming — for in the words of Dana Burnet:

> Who dreams shall live! And if we do not dream
> Then we shall build no Temple into Time . . .
> . . . Say nevermore
> That dreams are fragile things. What else endures
> Of all this broken world save only dreams!

WHICH ARE YOU?

Many women have said to me: "I've always wanted to hook a rug and I'm going to some day." But it is the woman who says: "I want to hook a rug. How shall I start?" that I am most interested in. The first is usually a dreamer — the second is a realist. And I like action!

The strange part of it is that this urge often gets those who are sure they are immune to this craft. Years ago, a young wife dropped into a neighbor's class, and brought her crocheting (a tablecloth). She scoffed at the rug work and said: "I much prefer to crochet." Yet she frequently left her work to watch progress on the rugs. As they were disbanding, she said: "Don't laugh now, but I think I'll try one rug — just ONE, because I must finish my tablecloth." She's been making rugs ever since — beautiful ones — and the tablecloth is still unfinished.

Hooking is not difficult, and can be very creative. By the simple process of pulling little strips of colored woolens through the mesh of burlap, you create a rose, leaf or tendril. These bits of color become very precious to each rugger! They store them away like gold, and usually know just where to find each piece of material which happens to be the exact color they need at the moment. Just try to get such a precious color away from them! "You may have my blood, but not my rags," they say.

> "Yes, Judge, I suppose I am guilty,
> But please let me tell you why,
> I'd been making a hooked rug, a big one,
> And it was done, all but a few square inches,
> When I ran out of material
> And could not match it anywhere.
> When I saw this man's coat
> I knew it was a perfect match . . .
> Everything went black . . .

When I came to, a cop was grabbing me,
As I ran down the street with the coat,
(It's a perfect match!)
Your Honor, if I plead guilty and go to jail
Can I keep the coat?"

And so this urge to create becomes a dominant possessive force. If you make the effort, you too, can find time to hook and fulfill this wish of your heart. Don't let hooking be driven into the background of your life through a complex of being too busy. Think over the needless duties or occupations which sap your energies, and spend that time on this creative work. Set aside and respect that hour or two when you can be alone with your thoughts and your rugs. Abandonment of occupation is not rest — a mind vacant is a mind distressed. Lose yourself in this creative craft, even if you have to step lively to keep up with it.

Then too, think what you derive from your effort — not only the thrill of creating — but the satisfaction of adding something of your own personality to your home.

The great Ruskin said: "I would have our dwelling houses built to be lovely; as rich and full of pleasantness as may be within . . . and with such differences as might suit and express each man's character and occupation and partly his history." Isn't that just what you are doing when you hook? An artistic hooked rug gives an air of distinction to your room. It may be expressive of your character and when made of intimate and sentimental materials, it can be a part of your history.

If you are positive in your thinking, and are ready to begin any piece of handiwork once your interest is aroused, you MAY travel a long way beyond your own imagination!

This was the experience of one woman who became a teacher after she was 70 years of age. She made a lovely rug of this design #400 Gratia (38 x 64) and accompanied it to one of our Exhibits.

One of the subtle details she hooked into her rug was the grayish-mauve tips to her leaves in the corners, which reflected the deep rose shades in her roses.

Her enthusiasm for the craft brought many women to her home for lessons, for her own health was too frail to travel about to her pupils. They brought the outside world into her home, and made long hours seem like minutes.

This is an extremely simple scroll to develop, especially if you use several values of just one hue. Greens, like the leaves — or running to the extreme of blue-greens or yellow-greens, make it a restful rug in any room. And for more interest, the scrolls may shade from one to the other extreme — blue-greens into yellow-green knobs, with the yellow-green dominating in the leaves.

The flowers are very simple to hook.

The fluctuating background in the rug illustrated was either a spot-dyed material or two or three slightly differing values of one color hooked in a mottled manner.

BENEFITS DERIVED

Hooking is so satisfying! As one woman said: "Hooking is much more constructive and worthwhile than spending so much time playing cards. Instead of spreading questionable gossip about neighbors, our conversation deals with making a leaf 'turn over' or a petal 'curl'."

It is a wholesome craft which appeals to all the family. It is not unusual to have several members of the family hooking at the same time. But it is not always advisable to hook on the same rug. There is a personal pride of workmanship in the experienced rugger that conflicts with the newly interested rugger. One rugger may perfect her technique quicker than another. A wife was indulgent with her husband's curiosity to try hooking on her rug. Very soon, however, his work was finer than hers and he said: "You get yourself another rug because I hook finer than you do and I don't want you to spoil *my* rug!"

When the youngsters show a desire to hook, set them at a piece all their own. It is good for the young to learn a craft at an early age. One of the prettiest sights I've ever seen was my little seven-year old granddaughter Jane bending over her frame, diligently hooking a pansy footstool. It has made her conscious of the "whiskers," ruffled edges, and the "nose and lip" on every real pansy she sees. It has taught her appreciation of another's work. "Oh, *that's good*, Grandma," she will say about the leaf in my rug, or stopping to look at Aunt Tibby's rug: "My, you do fine hooking, Aunt Tibby," she'll say, as she rubs her fingers across the surface.

It is a comfort and solace to the aged, for they often have many lonely hours to fill. "Time just flies when I hook," they'll say. To the physically handicapped, it is indeed a boon. One of my greatest thrills was to see the progress made by a dear friend who is a spastic. She has become so proficient that there is always someone eager to buy her rugs the moment they are finished. And now she is teaching the craft to others. It teaches perseverance, and this, when harnessed to courage, can produce wonders.

One of my letters tells of a Commander in the Navy, paralyzed for months. He watched a rugger hooking — expressed a desire to try it, and finally won in forcing his hand to move in the same manner. Eventually he walked! The following Thanksgiving his family breathed a silent prayer of thanks while they watched him face the test of carving the turkey and serving the dinner. Sure, of course he went back into the Navy! But he gratefully hands an "orchid" to his hooking teacher who encouraged him in his first great struggle.

Losing one's self in the craft is a great mental benefit. A few years ago a distraught husband appealed to a teacher on behalf of his wife, who had been going in and coming out of a mental institution for years. Did she think that she could perhaps interest his wife in hooking while "she is out this time"? Sure enough she loved it, and became an adept pupil. True, she had no interest whatever in her housework, but was so content and happy while hooking that her husband was overjoyed. That was several years ago, and she hasn't "gone back" yet.

Once you become a rugger, you'll find a new subject for conversation which will never wane — especially with those who share your interest. I don't know any topic which will hold out longer. "I should think you'd get tired of talking hooked rugs," some of your friends may say — but you never do!

Teachers have formed delightful associations with their pupils or with other teachers when they meet at various Exhibits. They can talk rags and rugs, scrolls and color blendings till the wee small hours of the morn.

So these are only a few examples of what happens when one is "bitten with the rug bug." A whole new world awaits you. You've really never seen all there is to see. Now you'll notice every flower. Every design and color will take on new meaning to you. Start a scrap book early, and don't hesitate to cut out the colored plates from your magazines, (after all, you paid for them). You, like thousands of other women, will find in this creative art, some of your happiest and most contented hours.

Then there is another benefit — perhaps not recognized as a part of this rug lure — but one which you and your family will soon appreciate. Your sense of humor begins to quicken.

It usually happens through a wider association with other pupils in class. During class day you forget your own cares and responsibilities in the fascination of learning how to use color. Then you begin to "tune in" on the conversation around you — and strange to say, it seldom includes gossip. It is most often experiences with hooked rugs in general, and obtaining material in particular. Often — probably because ruggers are so happy while hooking, infectious laughter spreads throughout the class. You'll find yourself thinking: "Why I haven't laughed like that for a long time!" And you'll find yourself searching for some funny things which may have happened to you too, to share with others — like this one which comes from California. A group of three eager ruggers were in a rag merchant's shop in search of their booty. Boxes and barrels of old clothing filled the shop. They bent and stretched into the barrels for coats or dresses of unusual mixtures and shades, often coming up with one, and sometimes tearing and sharing it with the others. On top of one barrel was a beautiful tweed coat of unusual pattern and tone. They all spotted it at once! "Oh, I'd like a little bit of that"— and so with a good strong pull the sleeves were torn from it and the coat was shared among them, just as a man came dashing into the room with a frantic look upon his face, saying: "Did you ladies see my light coat I laid down here?"

THE TOOLS

The requirements for making a hooked rug are few: a frame, (preferably an easel frame) . . . a good design . . . a small, fine hook . . . and some woolen rags. You'll have more fun if you will dye, but you can buy dyed materials, if you prefer.

FRAME: By all means start with a good strong frame. If you do, it will probably last a lifetime and be a constant satisfaction. The frame I recommend and sell will hold any rug up to 40 inches wide. It is stained light brown, beautifully made with brass plates, and rubber pads on the bottom. You need not hesitate to use it in your living room. It comes apart easily so you can put it into your car if traveling to class. These frames are always sent C.O.D. because of transportation charges.

DESIGN: DO start with a good design! Countless hours of labor are hooked into your rugs. They become an intimate part of your home (that is, if your children don't coax them from you) and if you choose a good design you will never tire of it. The cost is only a small fraction of the value of your finished rug. On the other hand, a poor design can never be redeemed by either fine technique or beautiful coloring, and it materially affects the value of your handiwork.

If the history or background of a design appeals to you, there are many of my old patterns which will intrigue you. But to many, the size of the rug, or the decoration of the room in which it is to be used, is of equal importance. Any design is enhanced if it is the proper size for the space in which it is to be used. So consider the position in which it is to lie, and then choose the approximate size in an APPROPRIATE design for your type of furnishings.

HOOK: Why is a small, fine hook necessary? Because you are going to cut your material very fine and you are pushing your hook into the mesh of the burlap to pull this fine strip through.

Therefore if your hook has a fat shank it will open up the mesh too far and will not hold your material firmly. The hook I recommend is a hand forged one with a slender shank and small handle, and it has my name on it.

Of course there are additional implements to make your hooking easier. Instead of straight shears, we use rug shears. The handle is slightly tipped up, allowing space for your fingers when cutting ends even with your loops. There are cutting machines which save precious time for hooking, especially if someone in the family will cut your material for you. They will slit your material into several lengths of the desired width. Although there are many types on the market, the two types I offer have been judged the best by impartial expert opinion. One is a precision instrument, it cuts 6 strips at a time, is ready at all times with no adjustment necessary, and comes in various widths. You choose the width that best suits your hooking. The other has interchangeable blades and comes in two sizes, one cutting 3 strips at a time and the other cutting 6 strips at a time. I'll gladly send you an illustrated folder with further descriptions of both machines, upon request.

There is also the burling iron (like a large tweezer) with precision points, excellent for pulling out loops when you are not pleased with an effect.

MATERIALS: Any woolen material can be used in hooking rugs, but I beg of you, do not mix it with cotton, silk or yarn. You are putting a lot of labor into your rugs. If properly made, they are good for a century. So do be careful and use only wools, and your rug will wear alike all over. The material may be old or new, from light weight dress woolens to a heavy coating. The latter, of course, would have to be cut extremely fine.

Materials which have a diagonal weave, such as tweeds, or those with a little pattern, will often produce a much more interesting effect when hooked, than plain materials.

Checks and plaids give another unusual effect, and in simple scrolls can be used as a "filler." Paisley shawls are perfectly beautiful in scrolls — and to what better use can we put these treasured old shawls? It is a way to preserve them for another century. Baby flannel or tropical blanket material is so soft and fine it makes lovely flowers. Old white flannel trousers can be tinted for backgrounds. Woolen bathrobes soften into lovely tones from frequent cleansing.

If you use jersey, mix it with other materials, to lose the otherwise loopy effect. In fact, I like to mix all my materials, whether in backgrounds or design. You then lose the uniform looped effect which one kind of material gives, and achieve an interesting texture to your rug.

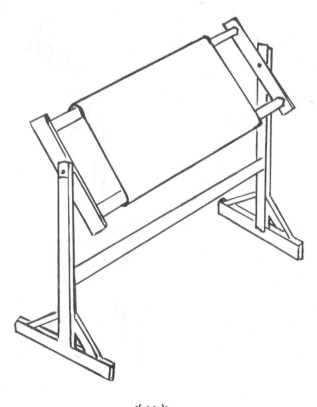

PREPARING THE PATTERN FOR FRAME

There are three ways of finishing a rug. One is to turn your burlap back an inch and hook through this double thickness, in which case your edge will be finished when the rug is hooked. If you prefer this way, cut the burlap one inch beyond the outside black outline on the pattern. (And I beg you to follow this outline, for if you hook more than an inch beyond this line you will throw the whole design out of proportion.) Fold and fell down with stitches about ¼ inch apart, being sure to catch in any fraying thread.

The second way is to stitch a tape, the color of your outside background, to the right side of your pattern and thumb tack it back out of your way (on the frame) until your rug is finished. Then cut your burlap 1½ inches from the hooked edge and make a hem about 1 inch wide. Now turn your tape back and hem down over the burlap hem. This facing will take the wear instead of the burlap hem, and it can be replaced when worn — whereas the burlap hem, once frayed, is gone, and the edges of your rug are doomed to constant mending.

The third way is to follow both of these procedures, stitching the tape at the edge of the rug. Then cut the burlap one inch beyond the edge of pattern, fold back and fell down, as suggested above. Tack the tape back out of the way on your frame, and hook the double edge right up to this tape. When your hooking is finished, hem the tape down on the back of your rug. I have come to believe that this is the best way — first because it gives you the double strength of burlap at the edge of the rug, and second — the tape turned back from the right side of rug protects that tiny exposed edge of burlap at the edge of your rug, which is its most vulnerable point.

Of course if your rug is round or oval, you cannot hook the edge double, and must follow the second way, of stitching tape all around the circular or oval outline on the right side of the pattern, easing it in on the curves. Now baste this binding back on the pattern, so it will be out of the way while hooking the detail. Mount it on your frame as though it was a rectangle. When it is finished, cut the pattern 1½ inches beyond the outline, hem, and lay the binding back over this hem, felling it down so that the tape makes a neat facing on the back of the rug.

You can treat the corners in two ways, if you are hooking a double thick edge:

(1) Cut corner, as in (A), leaving about ½ inch between the corner of the black outline (B) and the cut edge (C); fold corner back, as in (D); fold one side down and overcast as in (E). Do the same to the other side, and then overcast along the diagonal line, as in (F). This gives you a neat finish and does away with several thicknesses which you would otherwise have in the corners.

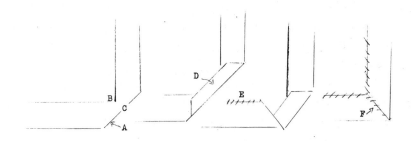

(Reduced in size)

(2) Or, after folding back on the outline, mark where the four thicknesses come together and cut a piece away from the corner, as in (G). Then overcast, being careful to whip the outside edges together closely, as in (H).

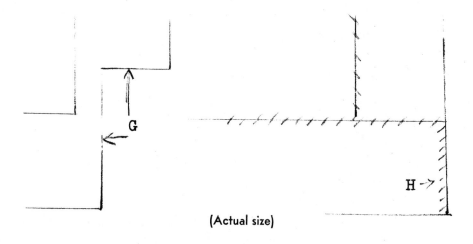

(Actual size)

Thus you will avoid four layers at the corners. It gives a neat appearance and extra strength to your finished rug.

Now that your pattern is all prepared, mount it on your frame. Here again, there are many ways of preparing your frame for the rug, but to save confusion, I will refer to only two ways:

(1) Wind the horizontal poles with some good strong material. I like a heavy grade of black sateen (it will not show the soil). Tear it across the width in about 3-inch strips. Turn one rough edge in and fasten it to the pole with a thumb tack. Now wind it in a diagonal fashion, turning one side of the material as you wind, so that all exposed parts will have a neat appearance. The strips may be sewn together before starting to wind, or you can fasten the end of each strip with a thumb tack and continue winding. Be sure that the final end is turned in neatly and fastened with a strong thumb tack.

Sew the edge of one end of the pattern to the square edge of the horizontal pole, using a double strong thread and making your stitches rather close but loose, so that there is a slight separation between pattern and rod, like (J):

Remember that you must be able to hook to the very edge of the burlap, and you'll need room for the fingers of your left hand

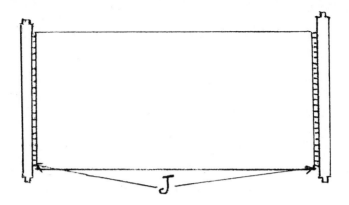

to feed the material to the very edge of the pattern. Sew the other end to the second pole, being very particular to attach it in the exact opposite position, so that as you wind your pattern from one pole to the other it will pull evenly.

(2) The other way is to tack a good strong, tightly woven material (bed ticking is good) all along each rod, having it long enough to wrap around the rod once and extend an inch or two beyond. Stitch a straight hem on the free end and sew your pattern, as described above, to the edge of this material.

Since it is important to keep the pattern taut as you hook, you should tie it to the side pieces. Nylon or silk stockings cut lengthwise in inch strips will stretch out thin and not make a hole in your burlap — yet they have enough substance to grasp in tying a bow knot, and are easily adjusted when it becomes necessary to wind from one pole to the other. Hook these strips through the double edge of the pattern, about ¼ inch from the edge, spaced about 4 inches apart. Tie to the edge of your frame. If you pull them too tight, you will make peaks. One way to avoid this is to run a knitting needle inside the edge and then tie from the inside of the needles. Or several small battery clips may also be used at regular intervals to grip the sides of the pattern. Remove the screw in the end and insert a shoelace or heavy cord through it and tie these to the side pieces of your frame.

TECHNIQUE

I am not in sympathy with those who feel that a hooked rug must be coarsely hooked and of crude design. Nor do I agree with the statement often made that all old hooked rugs were hooked that way.

"Lucy Baker"— a century-old rug, was so finely hooked and carefully blended in color that it became, with age, as soft and fine as velvet. This proves that in the olden days there were women who were not only artists, but who hooked their rugs with meticulous care. It was the expression of the individual!

So work with care, skill and artistry, that *your* handiwork will be a credit to you long after you are gone.

Hooking isn't difficult! In fact, hooking the loops through the burlap is quite simple, but you must have enough perseverance and interest to keep them close and even to produce a uniform effect.

First, cut some rags. It is important to keep a straight edge as you cut, for if you get off on a slant your material will pull apart easily. Tear your material in strips of about an inch or two wide and this will keep you straightened out. Cut these strips as narrow as possible and still have the material hang together (usually about ⅛ inch wide). If it is a heavy, closely woven material, you can cut it extremely fine—but if it is loosely woven, or very thin, you can cut a little wider. The finer you cut, the more detail you can bring into your design, but remember that straight edge! Of course a cutting machine will be a time saver and will aid in producing a uniform technique.

My hook fits easily into the palm of your hand, or if you prefer, it may be held between the thumb and forefinger, like a pencil. I like the palm hold best, but YOU hook whichever way is the easiest for YOU.

Be sure you are comfortable at your easel, so that there is no strain or tension in your position. Now relax. Do you know HOW? Sometimes a woman will say: "Hooking gives me a crick in the neck," or "an ache in the back." It's because she holds herself tense. When you sit down to hook, sit properly — well back in your chair. Now straighten your spine and square your shoulders. Rest your right arm on the horizontal bar of your frame, your left hand resting in your lap. Now breathe deeply a couple of times and relax all over — let every muscle go, your head dropping naturally over your work. For a few moments keep your mind on retaining this perfectly relaxed feeling — then start to hook. The moment you feel any tenseness, go through this little exercise again. Soon you will acquire the habit of hooking with utter ease.

Now start! Hold your left hand under the burlap with a piece of material held lightly between your forefinger and thumb, holding your fingers closely to the burlap. Push your hook through the mesh of the burlap, feel for the material between your fingers and pull the end through so that it sticks up an inch above the burlap. This beginning, and also the end of your strip, must always be brought to the top of your burlap. (When your rug is finished, all these single ends will be so closely fitted in between the loops that you will not be able to find one, and the strips cannot be pulled out). Now slip into the next mesh with the hook and pull a loop through this time, keeping it low to the burlap, your left hand fingers acting as a tension upon your strip. If the loop is too high, pull it back lower. Continue this operation, each time watching that the loop is pulled through exactly as the one before it, so that all the loops will be the same height. When you reach the end of the material, pull the last loop through so that your end and the beginning can be cut even with the loops. (Those shaped shears, permitting space for the fingers, are wonderfully convenient in cutting these ends. If you ever use a pair, you will never be without them again.) At first you may find yourself counting the meshes — slipping into each one, but soon you will work unconsciously, your main idea being to keep the loops close and even.

Why do I cut fine and hook low?

Because when you cut coarse and hook high, you form a brush-like effect, and all the grit from shoes falls in between these loops and down into the burlap, which wears the burlap and hence the rug. But if your loops are fine and low you have formed a close nap and the grit lies upon the surface of your rugs and can be quickly picked up with your vacuum. Yes, of course you can use a vacuum on your rugs IF you will be sure that all ends are pulled to the top surface of your rug.

You will note that I do not clip my loops. True, many of the old rugs were clipped, but it has been my observation that those which were not clipped are in the best condition today. Besides, an unclipped rug produces a clearer line to the design.

Every design presents its own particular problem, and will be discussed at greater length later. But there are a few simple fundamental rules to follow in most patterns:

Do not outline leaves and flowers in black.

Do not use one solid color in a flower or leaf.

Do not hook in straight lines, except in a geometric, or other designs made up of angular lines, or in following a border line.

Do use a variety of VALUES of one color in flowers, leaves and scrolls. They lend more interest to your rug.

Do vary your leaves — so they will not all be just alike.

Do swing your lines of hooking with the contour of your detail, to keep the beauty of a curve.

In background work, don't hook in straight lines (except in border lines), but hook in an irregular manner, like this:

Then follow these lines with other lines of hooking, as in (2), veering off at random, as in (3). Now you have formed little pools. Follow the contour of these little pools until they are filled. In this way, particularly if you mix your materials in texture and sometimes in SLIGHTLY DIFFERENT TONES, you will create some lovely backgrounds.

And as you work, frequently stand away from your frame and get a good light upon what you have done. This is the perspective you will have when the rug lies upon the floor.

DYEING

A beginner will often say: "I want to hook, but I don't want to dye. I'd rather make my rugs of the colors I have on hand." Well, just as an artist must mix and re-mix to get the tone or hue necessary to bring out a desired effect — just so a rugger must dye to achieve an artistic hooked rug. Of course if you have an UNLIMITED quantity of VARIED materials in countless hues, you might be able to get along without dyeing. But most ruggers do not have such a supply. So if you want closely shaded flowers and beautiful scrolls, you should dye — or be prepared to buy dyed materials. One pupil visiting her teacher's first exhibit, exclaimed over another pupil's rug. "What's wrong with MY rug; it doesn't look like this one?" she asked. "No," the teacher said, "it couldn't, because you won't dye!"

Since dyeing will teach you so much about color, aside from improving your rugs, I advise you to start dyeing when you begin to hook.

Which reminds me of a pupil who parked her car on Hallowe'en Eve near a friend's home and walked around the corner to see her teacher and arrange for a dyeing lesson. Pranksters let the air out of her tires! The policeman investigating, said: "Where is the owner of this car?" Her friend said: "She's gone to make an appointment to dye." He scratched his head in bewilderment. "And how long since a woman has to make an appointment to die?"

You can dye any colored material except black. Of course white will take the real hue of any dye in its full strength, or by using it in miserly fashion, in tints and weak shades.

Gray material will soften any hue. Grays of all kinds, plain, tweeds, mixtures, checks, plaids — if light — may be used for soft shades of any hue, and if dark they take on a "grayed" hue if in a weak dye, or a rich, dark hue, if the dye is strong.

Tans or medium browns, plain or patterned, will take on subdued shades of any dye. They absorb the color more than the grays. They are especially good when dyed any of the darker browns, like Light Brown, Golden Brown, Medium Brown, Seal Brown, Dark Brown or Mahogany, especially for backgrounds.

Bright reds may be deepened or darkened, and still retain some of their richness, if dyed in a weak solution of one of the green dyes. Any of the blue dyes will change bright red materials to rich purple and plum shades. Pink or dusty pink materials make lovely roses when dyed in Rose, Old Rose and Wild Rose.

Yellow materials dyed in any of the green dyes, make more lively greens, or dyed in any of the blue dyes, make unusual greens. A brilliant yellow may be dulled by tints of purple dyes.

Green material may be turned toward yellow-green by adding any yellow dye, or toward blue-greens by adding any of the blue dyes. If extremely bright, like Kelly Green, it may be dulled with any of the red dyes, or dyed in darker greens for backgrounds — or spot-dyed with blues and yellows, they work beautifully into all leaf detail.

Blue material dyed in any of the yellow dyes will give you some lovely greens, or in any of the red dyes, will produce some rich purples. Or you may turn them to blue-green in weak solutions of any of the green dyes. Brilliant blue may be dulled by weak orange dye.

I seldom dye purple material because it is so scarce, and often just what is needed for some particular flower, but it may be dulled in weak yellow dye.

Remember nothing is ever wasted in dyeing, for if it doesn't suit you it can always be put into another dye pot.

I have always recommended Cushing's Perfection Dye, because so far I have found it the best on the market. You never use the directions on the package, however, because you are not trying to get a uniform effect in your dyeing, but rather an irregularity or fluctuation in the tone, for this adds interest to the detail of the design. Thus I pack the dish tight with the material, and only enough dye bath to just see near the top. Thirty minutes boiling with a handful of salt (not table salt, but bag salt), or 4 tablespoons of vinegar to one quart of water will set the color. Be careful in rinsing, to use water that is gradually cooler than the bath. If you use cold water, it may harden or stiffen your wools.

In this modern age, much of the material we are using has been treated to be wrinkle or waterproof, and thus it sometimes resists taking the dye. Therefore, if you will immerse your material in a detergent like Cushing's Plurosol — before adding it to the dye pot — it will overcome this tendency.

There are also many special effects to achieve through dye — like "spot-dyeing," where you spot a material of one color with two or more dyes of other colors, so it is quite blotchy. (This is especially good in scrolls). "Casserole dyeing" where you add your layers of material, spotting with two or three dyes on each layer, will also produce some beautiful blends for scrolls. However dyeing is a special subject in itself and of too great a scope to do it justice here. I have already adequately treated this subject in "The Rainbow in Rags,"* which is every rugger's "Bible of color," and also specifically, through formulas, as applied to certain definite patterns, in the issues of The Dye Dabbler,* all of which are available to you. When you really get into the dye pot, your enthusiasm will amaze you. A pupil writes: "It is great fun to dye . . . the first pieces came out perfectly and I let out a cheer that brought forth my husband's remark: "I haven't heard you do that in years!"

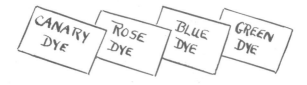

---

*A complete listing of all publications by Pearl K. McGown is to be found in the back of the book.

A CHAIR SEAT OR A RUG?

So often a beginner will say: "I guess I'll start on a small piece — a chair seat — or pocketbook." But I always say: "Don't! — learn the fundamentals of hooking on a small rug instead." Why? Because your chair seat or pocketbook is going to be much nearer your eye in use, but your rug lies upon the floor some distance away, and its discrepancies or faults are not so apparent. Furthermore, making a small rug does something for you. You feel a sense of accomplishment over making a rug — even though a small one — much more than a chair seat or pocketbook.

By the time you have finished a small rug you have become familiar with the feel of the hook. Its motion back and forth through the mesh becomes more or less unconscious, and you have learned to make your loops even.

On the other hand, when you have learned to hook evenly and well — chair seats are a wonderful medium through which to practice on certain flowers. That is my reason for providing a monthly chair seat or other small piece on which you can carry out the suggestions I make each month in my Letter Service, in regard to a particular flower or detail. I usually have also a monthly swatch of dyed colors with which to develop this particular flower — so that you can put the instruction to immediate use through this chair seat and swatch.

This is an excellent medium for those training for teaching this craft, because they do not always have the time to hook a lot of rugs which would give them experience in hooking all the different details.

This Letter Service is a monthly publication (10 months a year, July and August excepted), dealing with one flower or other detail each month, and sometimes including a discussion covering a whole design. As an example, the instructive portion of the Letter Service on a double chrysanthemum, and reference to the monthly chair seat and swatch would read as follows:

"In this month's chair seat (50¢), its two large blossoms with buds and leaves are much like those in "Ollivia," "Concord" and "Old Colonial." I have already had it hooked (you'll see it at this year's Exhibit) from Hattie's swatches. One of bluish-purple, one of rosy-rust, and leaves of bronzy-green spot-dyed with plum with accents of soft gold and veins of light mahogany. She made them extra large so three of them (50¢ each) should do it. We used them against a creamy home-spun blanket background. M-mmm — it's lovely! The flower swatches have 4 shades which I'll refer to as dark, medium dark, medium, and highlight.

Hook only one petal at a time so you can keep clearly in mind just what that particular petal is doing. For instance, petal (1) curls down away from the "cup" of the flower, turns over and back up, overlapping the base of the "cup." In this one use darkest shade at (A), highlight at petal's edge as indicated by dashes in (B), medium dark near base of petal and where it curls up, as in (C), and medium to fill remainder, and blend into the highlight.

Where a tip curls back over itself, use darkest at (D), highlight edge as in (E), medium dark at curve of petal (F), and blend medium into remaining space.

Where the center petals curl tightly, use highlight at edges and darkest shadow at center as indicated by shading in (G).

In other petals, first edge with highlight to preserve shape, shadow its darkest spots and shade medium dark into medium, always hooking with the contour of the petal.

The shading in the illustration shows where darkest tones should be, but if the base of the "cup" does not appear dark enough when you get through, squeeze in 2 or 3 loops of black (for bluish-purple one) or dark brown (for rosy-rust one) where I have placed tiny crosses.

In its bud, use dark on stem and at base of sepals as shaded in (H), and a bright lighter green in circle and in remainder of sepal, as in (J). Dark flower shades are indicated by shading. Use highlight or medium at edges of petals, filling with medium dark or medium.

Chrysanthemum leaves have already been discussed in the October 1944 issue. However, we developed these by using the darkest of the rosy-rust for the lower veins, and the light mahogany (in leaf swatch) for the upper ones. We tipped the points of the leaves marked (L) with soft gold, and those marked (M) with the dark rust of the flower. We used the darkest green from the leaf swatch to irregularly shadow the veins as indicated by (N). Intermediate green filled the remainder of leaf to pull shadows and accents together."

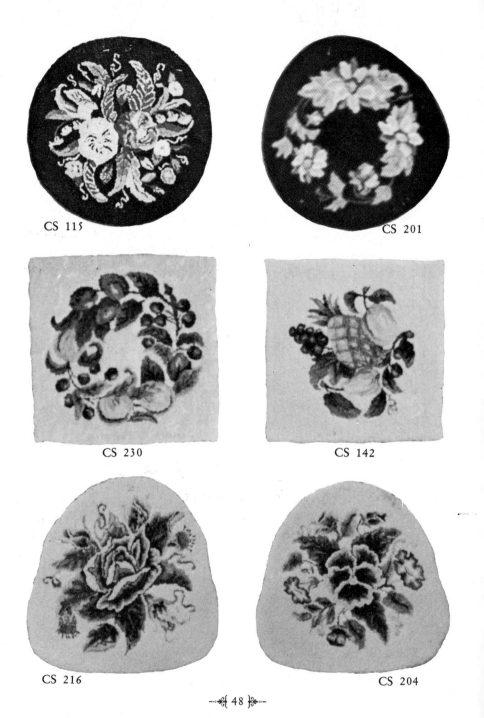

CS 115

CS 201

CS 230

CS 142

CS 216

CS 204

CHAIR SEATS

The round chair seats may be made for individual chairs, or a set of them for dinette chairs.

Consideration of the chair itself, and of the colors used around it, should dictate its color plan. If you are hooking a set, the backgrounds should all be the same. The detail may vary in each design if desired, but the proportions of the detail and the space it covers should be similar, so that there is a feeling that each is a part of a whole. Therefore there are several patterns which may be combined for this purpose. Even though the flower detail varies — there should be enough similarity or repetition in coloring in all of these to stamp them as a *set*.

Dark backgrounds dramatize the hues, as in #115 and #201.

The round chair seat may be squared off, as was done in #230 and #142. Instructions for hooking the peaches, plums and cherries in #230 are given on page 117.

A shaped seat is often desirable. Many of the chair seats have outlines suitable for Windsor and similar chairs, but if not, new outlines can be drawn upon them. They should always be in good proportion to the detail, as was done in #216 and #204.

Note the extreme highlights on the curled petals, in the realistic rose of #216.

There is a chair seat for practically every subject of the Letter Service. Many others have pleasing combinations of flowers, fruits and leaves.

These chair seat designs lend themselves to other purposes. Those with a plain center, like #201, serve as a table top to hold a lamp, or a piece of bric-a-brac — and in either rounds or squares they make beautiful pillows. When the backgrounds are hooked in soft grayed shades, the same material may be used for the backs of the pillow.

No. 347   Oak Scroll

No. 511   Lush

BEGINNERS' RUGS

Probably the most simple design to begin on is one like #347 "Oak Scroll," 24 x 36. It is a scrolly leaf, not too realistic, with acorns in the corners. A medium brown background with light tan inner field makes a good foil for the varied greens in the scrolly leaves.

Note the delightful variation of values from the darkest shade in the corners to the extreme light hues at the tips of the curling leaves.

I like the way the medium background has been extended to the inner corners, thus giving the center field a diamond outline. There is a consistent feeling of continuity in the way the dark values have been repeated.

But, if in your enthusiasm, you insist on starting on a floral design, (and most people do!), then try #511 "Lush," 24 x 35, which includes a simple scroll border on which to practice.

In this one, a very dark background under the scrolls offers a chance to repeat the color of flowers in the edge of the scroll, filling it in with a soft hued mixed, contrasting material.

One which stands out in my memory had a shadowed center — that is, the light background was shaded a little darker under all the floral detail. It was subtle too, in that its lighter brown scrolls blended closely into the dark brown background under them — thereby throwing most of the attention to the floral center.

I once heard a city teacher say that many of her pupils in the School Vocational classes were not familiar with any but the most common flowers, (what a pity!), and therefore it was difficult to make them "see" the flowers as they worked. Thus this design, with its floral center of roses, tulips and morning glories, has been a popular pattern, not only with city pupils, but town and country as well.

No. 346   FLOWERETTE

No. 524   IT'S A CINCH

Some novices are so enthusiastic when they start to hook, they seek a pattern with a lot of varied detail, and when they are perfectionists in most everything they do, the results are surprising!

Sister Sylvia used #346 Flowerette (24 x 36) for her first rug — mainly because all of the flowers were picked from her garden — and being one of those perfectionists, her efforts were most gratifying!

This pattern provides an introduction to shading many types of flowers. You learn to make a rose, a lily, a dahlia, a pansy and others, all in one rug. It will also teach you to balance your colors, because — since each flower appears but once — you must use its same hue in another flower in an opposite or triangular position.

The scroll is simple, and may repeat your leaf hues.

But you can improve in your technique on an extremely easy pattern, like #524 It's a Cinch (24½ x 37½).

Plan its colors so that one of the flower or leaf hues is repeated in the small scrolls of the border. You will find that mixtured materials or plaids of hues that reflect the center detail will give additional interest to these scrolls. The background of the border under the scroll may be a contrast to the inner one — or be the same, separated only by the straight border lines that frame the scrolls.

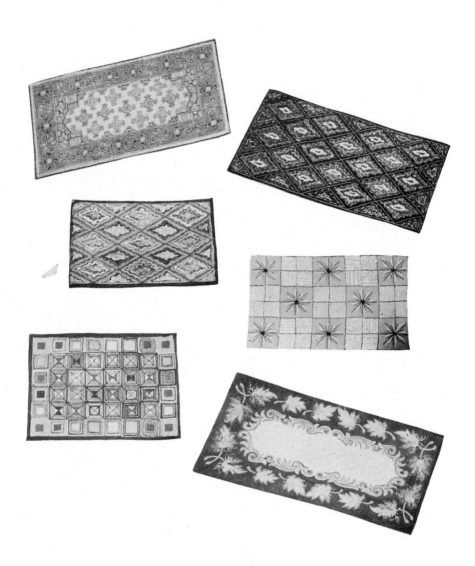

CAUTION! MEN HOOKING! LADIES, LOOK TO YOUR LAURELS!

Men love to hook rugs! The application of color is just as fascinating through the medium of woolen materials as through oils and water colors.

Some years ago, one of my teachers started a new class through a Woman's Club. Six of the women came back to their second lesson without their pattern, and all with a similar story. "My husband became intrigued with what I was doing — wanted to try it out to see how it worked — and ended up with the suggestion that I go back and start another rug, because he wanted to finish this one himself."

Men are very particular too, about their own technique. One husband openly flaunted his wife with the remark that she couldn't hook as evenly as he did — and frankly stated he did not want her to work on his rug.

Some men want detail in their rug — or a scenic design. But as a rule, they prefer leaf patterns (because of their reminder of the woods probably) or if there is enough interest to the design, geometrics or orientals. On these, once the colors are planned out they can go right ahead with the application of color.

The husky type of man who must be less active because of a heart condition or a nervous breakdown is often turned to hooking by his doctor who seeks a way to keep his hands busy and his mind at ease.

FUNDAMENTALS ON FLORAL
AND LEAF DETAIL

Here are some simple rules which apply to most detail of this type.

Generally, preserve the outline of your flower or leaf, by hooking its edge in the color you have chosen for it, before hooking within or around it. Then decide where its darkest shadow will be, and hook this next. Now visualize where the highlight might naturally be — if a flower, at the edge of a petal or where a petal bulges — and hook this next —and last of all use your intermediate shades — medium dark next to the darkest, and light next to the lightest, using your intermediate shades for the remainder — always swinging your lines of hooking with the contour of the petal. More specific examples will be shown under individual flowers. Don't be afraid to "let yourself go" on color, for we have to take some liberty with Nature in "painting" floral detail.

If a leaf, fluctuating values in its outline (best secured with spot-dyed material), are preferable to the hard line of contour which would result from using one solid shade. Next hook the veins of a contrasting hue or value. If the leaf is large enough and is to be shaded out to a decidedly lighter tip, lighten the extremities of the veins also. Then use dark values at the base of the leaf and along the lower part of the veins — light values at the tip — and finger your intermediate values into both, to pull the two extremes together. There are many other ways of developing leaves under a specific chapter.

You will find it much easier to blend and shade your floral detail if you will dye, unless you have an unlimited number of values and shades of one color which will blend. You will need from three to eight or more different values in your flowers, depending upon their size, and at least two in the tiny ones. Don't be afraid to use extremely light tints for highlights in petals, or very dark hues for shadows at the base of petals, where they begin to "cup." There should be at least three different values in a leaf, and usually many more. Stand away from your frame occasionally and get the light on your work. This is the perspective you will have when the rug lies upon the floor. Sometimes you can be too near your work to see it properly.

If you will not dye — or do not have the facilities, (but OH! what fun you miss!), SWATCHES are available for flowers, leaves and scrolls. These swatches are several strips of material of various widths and lengths, which contain the required number of values and intensities of a color, to make some particular flower, leaf, or type of scroll. Thus you may order roses, tulips, bleeding hearts, narcissus, and any number of other kinds of flowers. Small snips of the colors you are using in your rug, with a brief description of its background and other detail, will enable us to choose the proper colors.

Many ruggers will order swatches for a complete floral center (and sometimes the scroll) for a particular pattern, in which case, of course, one is assured of a harmonious development of color. In such a case, naturally, it is also advisable to have a brief description of the colors in the room where the rug is to be used, so that it will fit into the whole color scheme.

Estimates of cost are always gladly given.

Those flowers which you will find in most of the patterns are roses, pansies, morning glories, tulips, lilies, petunias, iris, dahlias, fuchsias, chrysanthemums, foxgloves and padulas. What is a padula? A padula is a flower that Grandmother planted in many of her old designs which none of us can quite identify. Any flower which cannot be named may be treated in a somewhat fanciful manner. The main idea is to have it harmonize with your other flowers, and become a part of your whole color plan. I will now tell you something more about each of these flowers.

ROSES

In working on a rose, develop only one petal at a time, for then you will not lose its detail, and will also be able to tell where one petal overlaps another.

For instance, suppose you desired to make this a deep wild rose hue. You should have at least five or six different values, with a wide variance between the darkest and lightest. You might use Wine dye for your darkest, Wild Rose for the medium shades, and Aqualon Pink for the lightest. Hook the Aqualon Pink irregularly around the outside edge of a petal, as in (A). Now hook the other extreme, a deep wine, a bit irregularly, at the base of the two foremost upright petals, to form a shadow, as in (B). Then use your medium wild rose shades, as in (C), to finger into these two extremes to bind them together. As you hook, picture in your mind the bulge of the petals which forms a "cup" around the stamens, and swing your hooking with the contour of each petal. Put character into each rose by accentuating highlights, extending them in some instances down into the intermediate tones, to form a bulge as in (D). The petals which curl back from the shadow lines will likewise shade lighter toward the petal's edge, and as you hook you will swing out and down with the contour of the petal as in (E). If the stamens are shown, as in this case, their color depends upon the color of the rose. A mixed goods with a black thread will give a speckled effect. Thus, a small check or plaid dyed chartreuse would make the stamens, depending, of course, on the color of the rose, but do not use a color which will attract attention to them. Now the center of this rose will be deep and dark, because the cup you have formed throws it into a shadow. So run your dark shadow tones between the stamens and the light edge of the two foremost upright petals and at the base of the two inner back petals as in (F), and use lighter (but not your lightest) tones at the edges of these rear petals.

In a rose where the center does not show at all and some petals simply overlap others, work from your darkest shadow at the base of each petal out to the lightest tone at the tip of each petal, but make the rear petals darker than those in the foreground.

If you lose the outline of your petal because your values are too much alike, pull in a very narrow strip of extreme light or dark (as necessary) where the outline should be. Don't be afraid to pull out and try again — failure really *teaches* us more than our apparent successes. We learn from the things we find we cannot do!

In making a very dark rose, your highlights may be rather sharp or brilliant instead of a very light tint, and your shadows may be a deep blackish red, navy or even black.

But there are other types of roses in my designs, and much depends upon whether you are doing what I term an old fashioned rose (like first one illustrated) or a more realistic one. So again, let's classify the minimum number of shades to use in this type.

(1) DARKEST, for shadows — usually a very deep tone.

(2) MEDIUM DARK — not as dark as the darkest but still a *deep* tone.

(3) MEDIUM — and this one should be the dominant shade of your rose and you'll use a greater proportion of it.

(4) LIGHT — perceptibly lighter than your medium.

(5) HIGHLIGHT — extremely light compared with your medium and light tones — or it may be a *brilliant* tone if the entire rose is a dark one.

In a full face rose, hook these five shades as suggested in (A). Be careful to accent the shadows at the base of the underlying petal with (2) and emphasize the highlight of the overlapping petal with (5), in order to pull the upper petal away from the lower one. Highlight each petal too, a bit different from the others, working it well back from the petal's edge to accent the highlight. Use a greater proportion of (3) for this is the tone you wish to dominate your rose. Keep thinking of the curve of each petal as you hook, and swing your shadows and other shades with the contour of the petal so you will make them "cup," and thus avoid the flat appearance you might otherwise get in a full face rose.

But if yours is a partly opened rose, like (B), use your gradation of colors as indicated in the illustration. This will give you a dark body with light rolling petals.

If you wish the body of your rose a very delicate color, with rolling petals of another hue, such as a white rose with rolling edges of pale pink — or a pale yellow rose with rolling edges of salmon, work the rose in reverse. That is, use your HIGHLIGHT in (1), your LIGHT in (2), your MEDIUM would remain the same, but (4) and (5) will be a light and medium shade of the second hue, which will be deep enough because of the delicate tone of your rose.

Delightful effects may be achieved by using a little imagination in working out your shadows and highlights. For instance, don't be afraid to introduce violet, salmon or rust in yellow roses, or pale yellowish-green, delicate yellow, shell pink or mauve shadows in your white roses. And in a white rose, like (C), try making the center of a deep color, such as rose-pink — or in a yellow rose a center of reddish-salmon. If you wish to give a light rose a little more color and character, tuck in some colorful shadow accents near the base of some of the petals as shown by the shading in illustration (C).

The placing of highlights —especially *patchy* ones — can do a lot to make your roses lifelike. Broad patches on the outside lower petal will make it curve back as in (D).

Highlights need not always be a lighter tone than the rose. In a dark garnet rose, for instance, the highlights may be an American Beauty shade (I am now speaking of color in terms of Cushing's dye), which because of its richness (especially if dyed over white) is enough different to form a highlight against the dark Garnet.

You can get an old fashioned effect by reversing the usual procedure of highlighting the edges of the petals. Instead, accent the edges in DEEP colors, and work down to a light base, as in (E). But in this case, on the upturned petals in the foreground (F) the deep colors should also be placed at the base to make it "cup" under, and also as a contrast to the lighter base of the petals which turn back (G). Be careful though, and see that the darker edges of the petals always lie against the light tones at the base of other petals, to make your rose "come to life." In its center try 2 or 3 loops of black for the stamens, (or a black and green check) and surround them with a few scattering loops of palest green.

It is very easy to lose the lines of the petals while hooking, and suddenly you wonder where one petal starts and another stops. Therefore, do one petal at a time when possible, and if some part of another petal overlaps it, pull in the color of the overlapping petal so that you can see in advance the effect it will have upon the petal you are working on — but be careful not to *pack* your hooking too close in doing a single petal, or you may crowd one out and exaggerate another.

Buds are tricky sometimes. If you want your bud to "twist," run highlights from base to tip, broadening it near top as suggested by (H). Flank on one side with your darkest tone. Use this dark tone at the top to indicate the closed petals, and also half way up the bud, as indicated by the shading, and then shade the highlights gradually into the intermediate shades in the remainder of the bud.

Sometimes you'll find little pods in my designs (the base of the rose after the petals have dropped away), as in "Wayside Memories." Shade the pod, placing a highlight in center of bulbous base, as illustrated in (J). Use a dark reddish tone for the dried sepals, and very *violent* reddish-orange for the stamens, capping each one with 2 or 3 loops of bright gold. They require these strong colors because of their small detail, for otherwise you might lose them in the background.

Now don't limit yourself too much to Nature in deciding upon the colors for your roses. It is much more important that your rug be harmonious with the draperies and furnishings in your room than that its roses be of *realistic* color. This is true of all flowers in your rugs.

Have you ever tried Terra Cotta and American Beauty, (and again I speak in terms of Cushing's dye) for the general tones of a rose, with shadows of Maroon, and highlights of Aqualon Pink — or a Canary Rose, with colorful accents and shadows of Scarlet and Orange (dyed over tan) and creamy white highlights — or a Crimson rose with shadows of Scarlet and Maroon, and a tint of Crimson for highlights — or a Mahogany Rose with shadows of Wine, and highlights of Pink and Rust? They are all a little out of the ordinary.

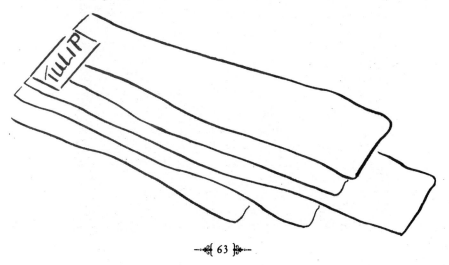

No. 288   MACKAY SCROLL

Probably one of the easiest designs on which to learn how to shade a rose is #288 Mackay Scroll (34 x 66).

You will note in the illustration how the shadows at the base of each rose help to "cup" it, and the extremely dark center suggests the effect of small petals clustered tightly together.

The scrolls you will notice are outlined with a light value and apparently filled with a slightly darker value. But I'll wager that if you were to see this rug you would find that two or three closely graded shades were used between the outline and the one which forms the darker area, for the transition appears to be extremely subtle. Notice too, where one part of the scroll lies over any other part, that the highlighted edge is used to separate them.

All of the leaf detail is extremely simple, and the design as a whole presents no color problems.

A complementary contrast between the roses, leaves and scroll would be pleasing. Thus your leaf greens would be the safest hue to use in the scroll if this is a first rug. The long sprays of leaves in the center may be a lighter value than those around the roses.

An extremely dark navy or black outer background with a medium light gray inner background would be good with roses in any of the reds, with either blue-green or yellow-green leaves and scroll. Or, an extremely dark dull green outer background would be good under a much lighter green scroll.

Rose-buds are fascinating to hook — you can give each one true individuality! They crop out from the rose leaves which form a delightful border in #469 Gift of Dreams (32½ x 66).

They may shade from a dark base to a light tip — or from a delicate base to colorful accents at the tip (like a Peace rose-bud).

Naturally they should all be of one hue, though of many values — to give continuity to the border. They should also be the buds of the roses in the center so there will be repetition of color to your color plan.

This particular design lends itself to a three toned background as shown in this illustration, but since there are three separate units of detail — border, scroll and floral center — keep it simple and somewhat neutral, to bring out the beauty of the coloring in the detail.

The spot-dyed material used in the intermediate background has given an interesting note to its large area.

The rug to the left is #87 Belmont Scroll, illustrated elsewhere in this book.

The coffee table (made from an old fashioned picture frame) was the clever idea of one of my teachers, and the design beneath its glass top is #481 Coffee Table Top (15 x 22).

Chair seats are often hooked in a large area to upholster an old fashioned chair like that to the extreme right.

WILD ROSES

The general color of your wild roses will be influenced by the color plan of your rug. Being a rug — you can, of course, take some poetic license with it. So even though Mother Nature's wild roses are usually white, pink and rose, if your rugs calls for something different, do not hesitate to use corn yellows, peach, salmon, or even delicate purplish-red. But whatever you decide upon, the principles of shading remain the same.

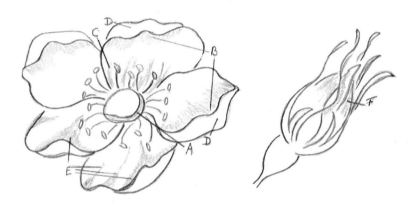

The main effect to achieve is to make the curled petals *turn over*, and this is done by contrast of values. Now the shade to be used to make them "turn" depends upon your background. If the petals lie against a dark background, a delicate shade will do the trick. But in such a case, proceed like this. Because we must not lose the center and its radiating stamens, hook them first. Use greenish-yellows for the center, running a dark shadow crescent line like Bronze, Mummy Brown or Purple around it, as in (A). Now pull in a couple of loops at each little stamen head of an orangey-yellow, or other color which will fit in with your color plan. Next run a shadow line or two of your darkest shades along the petal where it curls over, as shown by (B). At the base of the petal hook your lightest value, flaring the ends as in (C). Now finger a medium value down into the lighter tints, and a medium dark value up into your shadow line.

You can make your petals ripple if you run your next to darkest shade down toward the center, as in (E), and then go on and finger your remaining values into them. Hook the petal's turned over edge with an extremely light shade, and fill in, as shown in (D).

Of course if your background is light, you will have to reverse this procedure, using darker shades in the curled edges next to the light background. As you work, your own imagination will dictate various ways of shading your values to make your petals curl up and over. Aqualon Pink, Rose, Wild Rose, Maize, Salmon, Peach, or tints of the various reds or American Beauty are dyes which might be used for wild roses, but I would not rob you of the joy of giving vent to your own imagination.

If there are buds in your design, give them real deep tips and lighter bases (F).

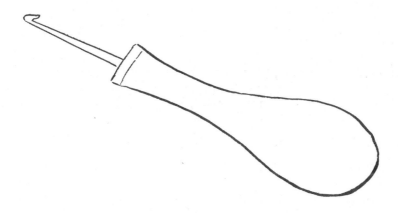

No. 488   WAYSIDE MEMORIES

No. 488   WAYSIDE MEMORIES

A pair of #488 Wayside Memories (30 x 50) is shown, so that you may study what happens to the detail against both extremely dark and medium light backgrounds.

You will notice in the one with the dark outer background the daisies stand out in sharp relief because of their extreme contrast of value to the background. In the other one the daisies are a darker value than the background and melt away into it.

Notice in the first one how the dark values are used at the edges of the morning glories which lie against the light inner background, while the half opened blossoms which lie on the outer background must be lightened at their edges to save their contour — though they may be shaded back into darker values within the funnel. Notice too, in this one that the daisies in the center which lie against the light background appear darker than those in the border, due no doubt to using many more dark shadows in the petals in order to maintain them against the light area surrounding them. All of the detail in this rug seems to be developed in a much more dramatic manner — in keeping with the sharp contrast of the outer background.

In the second one, the detail is not hooked in sharp contrasts of values, and therefore has the tendency to sink away and blend into the background.

When an all dark background is used, you get an entirely different effect from either of these.

TULIPS

A man stood watching a woman hook a tulip in her rug. "Where are your directions?" he asked. "I'm just hooking a tulip that's in my mind," she replied. And that's the way it often is.

Think of it — one day a blank piece of burlap and a bundle of rags, and at the end of another day a beautiful tulip blooms, and you find yourself walking back to the frame again and again, to scrutinize it — yes, and glory in it!

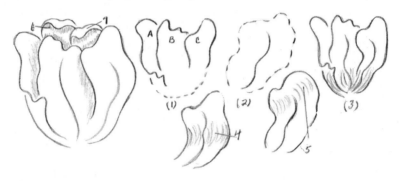

First, outline petals (A), (B), and (C) with the lightest shade of your chosen hue, to dotted lines, as in (1). Next use your darkest shade of the same color to hook the veins of the petals, as in (2) and to shadow irregularly around the base of the three petals, as in (3). Then use your medium shades, fingering them down into the shadows and flaring irregularly just beyond the middle of the petals, as in (4), and last, use a still lighter shade to the edge, as in (5). Always swing with each curve as you hook. Shadow the rear petals, as in (6) and use the next to the lightest shade on turnovers, as in (7). These same principles may be applied to shading your tulip in any two analogous hues, but you must have at least three distinctly different values, (such as *deep* purple, a *medium* mauve, blending into a *light* rose-pink). Be wary of strong, harsh, contrasting colors. But you may be quite dramatic and imaginative with your colors combined with gray and white, as those in "Florists Tulips." They have "flamed" or "feathered" colors — purple into white or rose into white. Look up "Flower and Fruit Prints" by Gordon Dunthorne, (probably found in your local Libraries).

When the tulip is much more open, as in (D), accent the feathered vein and the shadows even more, to get the feeling of depth — as shown by lines and shading.

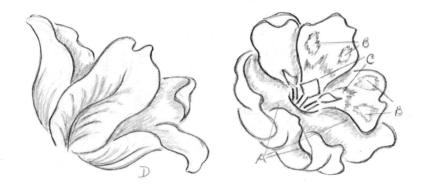

When the tulip has flared beyond its maturity, so you see more of the inside than the outside, place shadows on underlying petal where one lies over another — or where petal curls up, or where the edge of petal curls back and throws a shadow — all as in (A). Hook patchy highlights where a petal bulges or curls back, as in (B).

If your tulip is a dark one, blend your graduated shades back to a very pale or white sunburst around the stamens, as in (C). If your tulip is light, blend into a very dark sunburst about the stamens.

PANSIES

"And so I reach down in a bag
  Of pieces old and new
And dye some lovely pansy shades,
  Of colors grand to view.
And when I'm gone, I shall pass on
  Such beauty as I see,
My friends shall love the things I've loved,
  Because they're part of me."
                    — *Gladys Pattison*

Have you ever really noticed how much individuality pansies have? They are the most adjustable flower to color plans — for you can dress them in practically every hue.

Their petals may be monochromatic, the upper two possibly of a lighter or darker value than the other three, or they may be of two contrasting colors. Or the edges of the petals may be a contrast to the rest of the flower.

The whiskers may be extremely dark or delicately light, or very colorful against a pale or neutral petal.

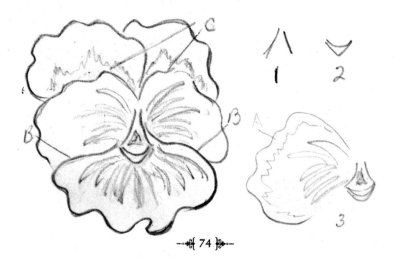

Hook the side of the nose first, with white as in (1), then hook a lower lip of orange-yellow as in (2), and fill the tiny center with yellow-green and one loop of rusty-orange. Next hook the whiskers in the three lower petals of the desired shade, flaring at the ends as in (3). Now to save the contour of the petal's edge, hook that next — either as an outline, or exaggerate it as in (A). Then finger your remaining shades into these accents and down into the whiskers. Sometimes you may have to lighten or darken the edges of the lower petal, at (B), to pull it from the underlying side petal. Now if you are going to make the upper petals lighter than the lower ones — use your lightest tone at the base of the petal as in (C) and hook out to edge. If they are to be darker than the lower petals — shadow them at (C) and hook out to a lighter edge.

Until your own fancy dictates their colors, try some of these, IF they fit into your color scheme:

Light brown whiskers, shaded into yellow lower petals with pale mahogany upper petals.

Light blue whiskers, shading into deep blue lower petals with navy edges, and upper petals of red-purple shaded into plum edges.

White whiskers, shading into pale blue lower petals, with deep old blue upper petals.

Plum and purple whiskers shading into white lower petals with upper petals of white with pale mauve shadows.

Purple whiskers shading into lavender lower petals, with yellow upper petals.

Wine whiskers shading into lavender in all petals with pale blue edges.

Brown whiskers shading into rose in all petals with broad pinky-white edges.

Gold whiskers shaded into rich purple lower petals, with weak gold upper petals.

Light blue whiskers shaded into purple petals, with light orchid edges and upper petals of medium and light yellow.

MORNING GLORIES

First visualize your Glory — will it have a light throat with dark rich shades near the outer edges — or vice versa? The background of your rug may influence your decision.

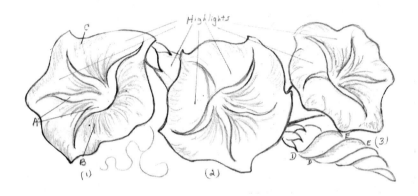

If a light throat is desired, use your tints in the throat, as in (1). They may continue to form the tapering veins if desired, as shown by (A). Then blend medium shades around them with darker shades at the edges, as shown by (C). In the petal in the foreground, use much darker values where indicated by (B), and shade out to a light edge.

If a dark throat is desired, reverse procedure, hooking from dark center into medium and out to light edges. But in this case, highlight the curled petal in foreground, as in (2), shading that part back to a darker edge. The base, shaped like a funnel, may be light if petals are dark, or vice versa.

Always hook with the curve of the petal, starting at the center, swinging out toward the edges. Highlights are important, and it's fun to achieve your own. They may fall near the edges in an irregular manner, as suggested in (1) or where the petals curl back as in (2), or between the inner and outer edges of the petals as in (3). Highlights have to be a bit extreme. Stand back and look at your rug frequently, remembering that what may seem exaggerated when your eye is within a foot of the rug becomes good perspective at a distance.

You can make the veins a definite contrast in color, if desired, like an American Beauty vein in a purple Glory.

The buds should twist by running dark shades from (D) to (E), following with 2 or 3 gradually lighter shades in the remaining part of each section, with a dot of the brightest color at the tip.

The tendrils usually found with glories may be light or sharp greens, golds, mummy browns and many hues, depending upon your color plan.

IRIS

The Iris was well named for the Greek Goddess of the Rainbow, who "wore a robe of a thousand varying colors."

Grandma called them "flags"— and almost never hooked them in her rugs — that is, so we recognize them — but perhaps they seemed too difficult. They need not be to you!

Well, let's hook one! Their "standards" (upright petals) and "falls" (the graceful side petals which curl back), may be made alike — or with light standards and dark falls — or vice versa, or in contrasting colors.

The veining in the petals may be stressed or not, as you wish, with darker shades, as in petals (1) and (2) — or you may shade from a dark area around the center vein to a light area at the edge, as in petals (3) and (4).

In any event, accent the central vein in the standards — for it helps to make the petal "curl." Where one petal curls or laps over another, use an extreme highlight on the overlapping petal (6) and use very dark shadows on the underlying petal (5).

On the "falls" the beard (7) would be hooked in first, of delicate canary gold, or deep orange, (depending on the hue of your Iris), and if the center is shown, as in this sketch, that should be colored likewise.

Be deliberately irregular in shading the petals, so that those on the side, or peeking from the rear, will have a darker effect — to throw them into the background and give a better perspective.

Yet you may sometimes have to use a slightly lighter or darker edge than the value of your background, to save its contour.

Sometimes a shadow may be a different color than the general hue of the Iris. For instance, a purple Iris could have a shadow of wine if it is not too bright. Likewise a light pink Iris might have a soft purple shadow. If you develop yellow Iris, give them character by using plenty of extremely light shades. Use only a small amount of the rich yellow, but plenty of shadows of Mummy Brown or any of the golden browns or even darker browns for veins and accents.

In white Iris, be lavish with accents of pinky-orchids or bluish-lavenders to give them character, with pure white as highlights. You can still achieve a "white effect."

No. 491 FLORAL BROOCH

No. 506 PERSIAN PARADISE

Iris appears in #491 Floral Brooch (28 x 50) and your whole color plan may be built around them, if desired. Their colors are easily harmonized with the wild roses and canterbury bells which are also prominent in this design.

The light and dark contrasts in both the scroll and floral center of the rug illustrated, are very pleasing.

Iris also appears in the center and corners of #506 Persian Paradise (38 x 56).

In the rug illustrated a feeling of "lace" has been given to the scroll border through the shadows and highlights. The whole rug has an excellent balance of medium dark and light contrasts in detail and backgrounds.

The dark rich shades often used in iris make good companions to similar rich coloring in the poppies which are rather dominant in this pattern. Avoid spottiness by using two analogous hues for them — for instance, a purple iris with a purplish-red (not orange-red) poppy.

But the room in which you are to use a rug will influence your whole color plan. Thus, in a bedroom where such rich shades might be inappropriate, white iris with purple accents may be bound to white poppies with gray shadows, and possibly to a whitish lace scroll. Such a development in white with colorful accents permits you to use more color in your background. Thus, the white iris, poppies and lacy scroll might lie upon a powder blue background, possibly slightly lighter on the inside.

Since this would make a rather "cool" color plan, you can balance this feeling with warm shades of yellows and corals in the rest of the floral detail.

No. 452   ELF'S DELIGHT

No. 153   MOONEY PANSY

If you enjoy hooking fine detail, #452 Elf's Delight (28 x 46) will intrigue you. Its ferny frond border lends itself to beautiful developments of bronzy-browns and soft yellow-greens or blue-greens. The floral center is made up of all sorts of wild flowers.

It takes the perfectionist to hook it properly! One of my California teachers brought her 11 year old granddaughter to my annual Exhibit. Being busy as a hostess, she suggested that her granddaughter examine all the rugs carefully, and choose the one she liked the best, promising to make it for her.

When asked if she had come to a decision, she said, "Yes" and pointed to a "Romantique" of soft subdued coloring. "So you think that is the most beautiful rug here?" Grandma asked. "Oh no," she replied, "not the most beautiful, but the most practical for it will fit into any living room with almost any colors I would choose. But the most beautiful one is that Elf's Delight!" She recognized the wonderful technique of a perfectionist!

Pansies in #153 Mooney Pansy (30 x 48) are one of the most popular flowers to hook. Since they are the dominant flower in this pattern, the daisies should play second fiddle, and never should be bright enough to demand first attention. Naturally, the center pansies should repeat similar colors to those in the corners. The corners may be balanced diagonally — or all made in similar colorings. The little lilies of the valley indicate the division line in case you desire to lighten your background within.

Play down the leaves — let them be simple and serve only to complement the colorful petals.

LILIES

Lilies are *tricky* — for most of them call for delicate tones and subtle treatment — and you *can* go astray. As one reader wrote: "Mine are just blobs!" Well, you've got to be imaginative, in order to mould and shape them.

In design particularly, flowers do not have to be too true to Nature. The important thing in rugs is the effect you get, especially when viewed *on the floor,* so you *must* take some liberties with Nature.

But even Nature shows almost no limitation in the hues of lilies. Pick up any flower book and among the sixty-odd members of the Lilium family you will find them reddish-orange, orange-apricot, mahogany, pink, gold, yellow, greenish-white, blue and mauve.

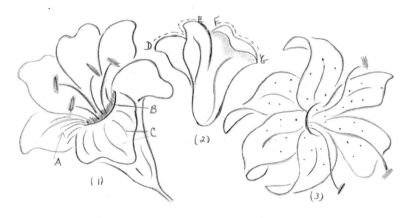

Let's assume you are making the Regal Lily as shown in (1). First put in your stamens. A Regal Lily, having a soft yellow throat, can take quite a gay bright green stamen. At the end of each stamen, pull in about 5 loops of mahogany brown for the pollen "caps." Now 5 loops may seem a lot for these tiny "caps," but I find that when the rest of the petal is hooked, these "caps"

shrink in size, and they must be definite enough to have character.

Now hook the throat in soft yellow as shown by the shading in petal (A), always flaring the ends so you can finger other colors down into them. Where one petal overlaps another in the throat, use a shadow of deep bronzy-gold on the *under petal* and use this again for a shadowy curve as in (B). Next outline the petal with some white "fuzzy-wuzzy." What is it? Well, it's any woolen material which has a little fuzz to it, so that when hooked, it gives a soft edge to the petal instead of a *loopy outline* that you sometimes get from a closely woven, smoothly finished material. Perhaps I'm queer, but I like "fuzzy-wuzzy" to edge the petals of any flower, but especially a white one. Now hook your mixed whites irregularly down into the yellow throat. Where the white part of a petal overlaps another, use a gray shadow on the underlying petal.

In any white flower, mix your white materials, because even in white there is a variety of *tones,* and mixing them breaks up the flat appearance you get in using a single white.

In the fore petal which turns toward you, highlight with the whitest fuzzy-wuzzy on both the edge and the horizontal curve where it disappears into the throat. Now hook your mixed whites in a graceful swinging manner as indicated by (C).

In the funnel part of the Regal Lily, and as shown in (2), use a deep rose-pink along the veins, flanking them half way up with soft yellow, and hooking the yellow into the base of the funnel. Use the white fuzzy-wuzzy on the flaring petals from point (D) around to about (E), using mixed whites to finger down into the base. Make your petal turn back by using pure white in the turn back, from (F) to (G) and shadow under the turn back with gray before using mixed whites in remainder.

In case the throat and petal are to be one color, *shadow* the throat with deeper tones to give *depth.*

Stamens depend upon the general tone of the throat, for if it is light, use medium dark stamens, but if the throat is a medium shade, your stamens will have to be much darker to have character. In a darker, or deep colored lily, however, the opposite is true — the stamens must be a very light contrast — a delicate apricot — a yellowish or greenish-white.

A "freckled" lily (3) always intrigues me! It has many possibilities in color, for instance pale pink with freckles of wine.

"Freckle" it by squeezing an end up through (after your petal is completed), making one loop, and cut. By being careful, you can slip into places between the loops of your hooking and get a good effect, but be careful not to have too many freckles.

Shadow the underneath side of the curling petals with darker tones. If desired, you can get a "crevice" effect to your petals if you use your darker tones along the center of the petal, shading it lighter toward the edges.

It's amazing how much life you can put into white lilies by *tints* of color, and still keep them white. Here are some ways of doing it. Dye very delicate splotchy tints of Maize, Aqualon Pink or Coral over white — rather far apart — and it must be only a mere suggestion of color, and use this to bring a warm glint into white petals. Or for Easter lilies, dye delicate tints of Olive Green and Buttercup Yellow over white or beige and use along the center of the petals, with tints of Silver Gray and Orchid for the shadowy throat.

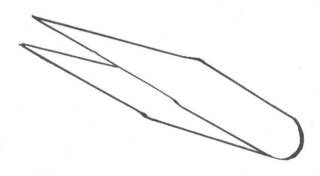

PETUNIAS

Who would ever think of our New England's favorite and prolific "Petunias" as originating in Southern Brazil?

When "painting" them into hooked rugs, use some license with highlights to get away from the solid effect of their monotone coloring. They seem to take on more character, too, when their funnels are either lighter or darker than the open blossoms.

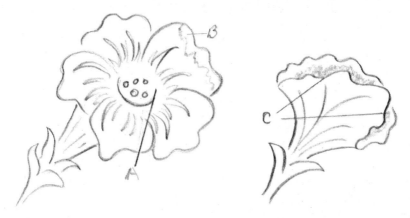

They may have a light throat, if preferred, as in (A). Use an extremely light shade of the color chosen — almost bordering into white, as shown by irregular lines around throat. Use a medium dark irregular edge, as in (B), with about two intermediate shades, (second lightest into lightest, second darkest into darkest), to pull the two extremes together, and always swinging your line of hooking with the curving vein in each petal.

The stamens, if they show, may be two or three loops of yellow, or a yellowish-green in the lighter blossoms, and in the purplish-blue or rose blossoms try a greenish-black. Sometimes the stamens do not appear at all.

If a dark throat is preferred, reverse this procedure.

If a petunia is turned in graceful profile, you must consider your background in determining its general tone. If on a dark background, use lighter shades at the edges of the rear petals, blending back to a darker shade, as indicated by sketch, and using your darker shades again in the lines indicated at the base. Then shade gradually lighter around these lines, blending into your lightest shade at the edge marked (C). Of course, if on a light background, reverse the procedure. There need be no bounds to your imagination in "painting" these petunias into your rugs in exactly the shades which will look best in your room. Give it rein! And then the same principles may be applied to similarly shaped, but not too realistic flowers, of Grandmother's designs.

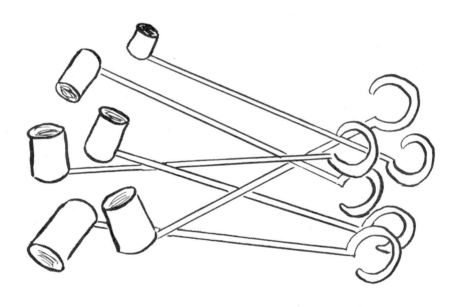

DAHLIAS

Dahlias! What memories they bring! Mother, saving her bulbs from year to year — she always loved the rich dark red ones, and there was always a dining room center piece of their small, tightly petaled blooms through the summer. "The smallest things make loveliest memories."

Use three values of one color — the first a very deep and dark shade as a shadow, where one petal overlaps another — the second a medium fluctuating shade, (spot-dyed) — the third a very light tint to separate the petals. Start with petal (1) as shown in enlarged sketch (B), first putting in the shadows *at the base* of the surrounding petals. Those shadows are short and broken and their irregularity gives a natural effect. Then outline petal (1) with the lightest tint and fill it in with the medium fluctuating shades — those fluctuating shades preventing the petals from becoming too uniform. Now do likewise with petal (2) and so on. Taking one petal at a time, placing your shadows in only the surrounding petals, is less confusing than putting in all the shadows at one time. After hooking the stamen center, run a shadow line of the darkest shade or a pleasing contrast half way around the center, as in (C).

FUCHSIAS

    Fuchsias with their jewel-like blossoms are treasured house plants to most of us. Once in a long time Mother had one, and it always took the place of honor among her broad leaved Begonias. How she did tend it to keep it blossoming! Perhaps that memory is why I love them so!

    Let's make these with fuchsia sepals and purplish corollas.

Outline the tube and sepals first to keep their contour, using your lighter tones, (unless against a very light background, when you may have to deepen the color). Where the sepals turn back against their own color, form a shadow with darker shades as in (1). Highlight as in (2) to give a sheen. Shadows may be placed for accent as in (3). After these highlights and shadows have been placed, use intermediate tones to bind all together. Be particular — especially in a curling petal or sepal, to swing your hooking with each curve to make it turn and curl.

Accentuate the highlight of one purplish petal, where it overlaps another, by a dark shadow (4). (Very dark!) Give each corolla a personality of its own through these shadows and highlights . . . In the buds use a deep purple for the peeping petals as in (5) . . . The stamens are often (but not always) the color of the sepals, and the little "caps" may be chartreuse or deep gold or the color of the petals, (or better still, the color which will show up on your background)! Outline the seed pod in bronze-green, with a loop of bright green in its center (6), to give a glossy or bulbous effect.

The veins of the leaves are quite colorful — often fuchsia. The foliage is very graceful with its curly green leaves, and WHAT a chance to let your imagination have full swing! They may be bluish-green, some of them running toward yellow-greens, while the smaller ones might be more delicate — almost a grayish blue-green. You know the underneath side of the leaf is often quite a contrast — sometimes a most delicate gray-green. Shadow some of them as in (A). Use rather bright yellow-greens as highlights, with shadowy tips on others as in (B), or let your highlight fall near the center of the leaf, darkening it where the leaf curls back as in (C). Combine yellow-greens and blue-greens in one leaf, the lighter yellow-greens along the upper edge, the deeper dark blue-greens along the lower side, as in (D).

There are countless other combinations of color — sepals of rose with purplish petals — or creamy white with rose-pink — or pink with lavender-white — or apricot with delicate orange — or delicate orangey-pink with delicate orangey-salmon . . . But don't be *bound* by these suggestions. They are growing in your rugs, not in your gardens, so use your imagination! The colors should be suggestive of the flowers but should also tie up to your whole color scheme. If a bluish-lavender petal with sepals of light peachy-pink are needed for contrast on a dark or black background, by all means make them that way!

SUBTLE ACCENTS IN ALL FLOWERS

Of course real artistry in all your flowers comes from your imaginative mind, as you hook.

It calls for a little daring — a trial and error method — but it often pays off well, and when successful, brings a thrill like no other in the world!

Following the suggestions of the Letter Service in forming any of these flowers is a fairly safe path until you become better acquainted with all flowers — and with color in general. Then be daring enough to veer off on your own path of discovery.

You'll gain courage to do this by a keener observation of detail in everything you see. And hooking rugs will develop this sense within you.

The better flower catalogs will open your mind to the combination of colors in all flowers. Flower prints will be closely scrutinized and reduced to terms of shadows, highlights and contrasting accents. Colored advertisements in the better magazines by artists who have planned to intrigue you, will suggest backgrounds and scrolls. Chintz and drapery materials are very daring in accenting shadows and highlights, and they will suggest new ways of using your materials.

A gradation of hues is very important if you are seeking a realistic effect — but imagination and daring in the use of color adds artistry to your work!

All of these things will help you to add a shadow here, or touch up a highlight there, which may give what I call "oomph" to your detail, and a thrill to your heart!

Pull in these little touches and stand away from your work frequently and see if you have given it that "something" which it needed!

A fuchsia, like many other flowers, may not always be too realistic in some of my designs, for sometimes the charm of an old pattern which has been sent to me for restoration, must not be lost!

This was so in #434 Tattle Corner Twins (41½ x 72), where the fuchsias are large, and quite bulbous at their base.

I have one of this design which I love, in my bedroom! In fact, it gave me the keynote of color to do over my room when I achieved another dream, and finally secured a tester top bed.

The soft somewhat grayed coral and sagey green in the scrolls against a very dark brown outer background, and a warm creamy inside background, fit beautifully into this room, covered as it was, with medium sagey-green wall paper.

The three large center roses were a delicate coral pink, a deeper shade of it and mahogany, and the fuchsias were an extremely deep plum-purple.

I intensified the coral of the rug by using its hue as a tufted velvet covering for some very old hand carved walnut chairs, and used it again in the ball fringe of my white organdy tester top valances and window draperies.

I'm sure your curiosity must be tormenting you as to how this design received its name. Well, the old pattern came to me from a little hamlet in Maine which was nick-named "Tattle Corner" — no doubt the neighbors kept tabs on what was going on in the surrounding area.

In the rug illustrated, #513 Exultation (34 x 60), the scrolls were developed of neutral grays with the darker shades near the base or flanking the veins, blending out into lighter grays and off-white tips. The darker grays are also stressed in the underlying curls, while the off-white highlights are accented in the twirling knobs. The veins of the scrolls repeat the rose-pinks of the roses, being darker in the midst of shadows and shading out to lighter tints at the extremities where the curls lighten.

In a flowered center in which calla lilies appear, be careful to use plenty of shadows among your whites, especially if working against a dark background. Otherwise, the whites will be too contrasting to the dark background, and will appear startlingly white against it. Light grayish-green, light lavender, or just light gray all make good shadows.

To lend interest, the other three lilies in profile might be developed as Regal lilies, and thus possibly repeat some of the deep pinks of a rose, along their funnels, as a tie up to the rose. Likewise, the yellow tongue of the calla might be repeated in a duller shade as the centers of the daisies, thus bringing repetition into the color scheme.

Another rug of this design which stands out in my memory was developed with a very dark brown center background — a medium soft brown outer background with just a few lines of the darker brown at the extreme edge. The scrolls were developed in light tannish mixtures and tweeds of slightly different values on each side of the vein that gave them a sculptured effect. Some of the tweeds leaned toward a light soft blue tone and these were massed in some of the curls to give them interest.

A lily provides the extreme light contrast against darker detail which makes a design most interesting. One of them appears in #385 Sally's Seashell (32½ x 54).

Its delicate accents of color may be repeated in some of the shading for the fanciful sea shell border. Thus, soft pinks and orchids used to give oomph to the lily might be used again to highlight the outer edges of some of the sea shells.

In a design of this type, where various units make up a border — and they range from leafy scroll to shell — give the whole border a feeling of continuity by repetition of colors, so there will be no sharp jumps or breaks in its development.

Thus the center leafy scrolls on the long side might be shaded in soft dull sea greens (possibly a reflection from some of the tips of the leaves in the center) and veined in purples and grayed pinks. The next shell might have deep dull blue-green shadows with a roll-over of lighter purple-blues. The corner shell might have dark accents of deep dull purple shading into grays and rolling out to lighter values, with colorful edges of the grayed pinks and orchids. The end scrolls might be in the same hues as the first shell, and so on around the border. The hues should all be grayed and their values should not be strikingly different — or they may interrupt the feeling of continuity. On deep dull blue-green or bluish-gray background they would be very effective.

Thus, even a lily may influence your entire color plan.

CHRYSANTHEMUMS

This "Chrys" is not the incurved type, but rather reflexed — a sort of shaggy bloom with curling petals. It appears in several of my designs, "Romantique" and "Gainsborough" being two of them.

It is often developed in bronzy-yellow or brownish-golden hues and in a desire to use light backgrounds the edges are often lost. In such a case use dark shades (but not as a stiff outline) at the edges of many of the petals.

They are lovely in soft Egyptian reds, Terra Cottas, Peach, Mahogany, Chartreuse and White. Because the petals are small and lie upon each other, you must rely upon considerable contrast between the lighter tones of the top petals and the darker shades of those beneath. You can bring more character into your blossoms too, if you do not cling too closely to light and dark shades of *one* color. Rather use some of the adjoining hues on the color wheel. For instance, in pink or rose petals, shadow with reddish violet, or in peach, shadow with terra cotta shades — or in yellow, shadow with goldish-green.

Hook only one petal at a time. Run your highlights along the edge of the top petals clear to the point, where it may turn, from (A) to (B), blending into slightly dark shades in middle of petal. Use your shadow tones for the under part of the petal (if it shows) as in (C), and make the change in value quite extreme — for there will be but a tiny bit of it, and unless it is quite extreme, it will not show up. Make those petals which are shaded — of your shadow tones. Just a line or two of the shadow tones indicated by my shading, (where a top petal overlaps another), will make that upper petal "stand away" from the other. Don't make every petal exactly alike. Of course you should use the dyed materials, and if they fluctuate, so much the better. Use dark tones along the base of those few tiny petals which curl about the stamen center. Pull some gay yellows and some bright greens into the little circles indicating stamens, and if your material is a mixture which has a black thread in it, it is just priceless for this sort of thing! Then fill in remainder with a medium or dark shade of brown or green.

In spite of their shaggy, small petals, chrysanthemums are very simple to hook, provided you get accent of highlight and shadow — making one petal overlap another by contrast of value. If the petals merge too closely near their base, hook in an extremely dark line next to very light ones, and it should "do the trick."

FOXGLOVE

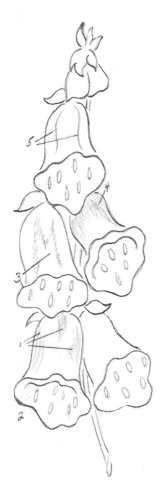

Fairy's Gloves or *Finger Flowers* to some, but *FOXGLOVE* to most of us, with their "pyramid of bells, gloriously purpled and white" are sometimes referred to as a "belfry for the fairies." Though Nature paints them in rosy pinks, violet and yellowish-creams — when we hook them in rugs — and especially when the balance of color becomes of more importance than even Nature herself — we make them blue and yellow too.

Let's put the accents in first — using a dark shade along the sides and in the center top as indicated in (1), but having a still darker value of the same color to run around the mouth of the open bell to form a *shadow* as in (2). Now jump from this extreme to the very lightest tone for a highlight, hooking it in an irregular manner — and also running it around the edge of the mouth of the bell as indicated in (3). We must now bind these two extremes together by filling in the remainder with a medium shade, which will be lighter than the dark tones, but much darker than the highlights, so that when completed, even though the highlights may seem extreme at close range, at a distance, they round out into bells.

The inside of the bell is freckled, and you must be extreme with these freckles, even using black when the bells are blue — or wine when rose-pink — or dark brown when light violet. To make freckles, pull your end through, make one full loop and cut on second loop. Your medium tones will fill the remaining space around the freckles.

Now don't accent all the bells alike — naturally all those on one stalk will be the same color, but vary the shades where one bell overlaps another. Throw a deep shadow over it by using much darker shades on the bell beneath, as in (4). You can also give them a more shaped or "creased" effect by running a streaked highlight with a shadow beside it to the top of the bell as in (5). Use light greens in the sepals, but vary these too, with darker tones along their outlines.

No. 389   Thalia

No. 508   Spice of Life

All of the flowers in #389 Thalia (27 x 46) are extremely simple to hook, and the variety of leaf detail will fascinate a beginner.

Several values of one color — providing they are somewhat soft and grayed — may be used in shading the scroll from a dark under curve to a light outer curve. Or its scroll may also gradually shade from extremely dark ends and corners to lighter extremities at the center.

Soft green scrolls on blackish-green outer background, or deep blue scrolls upon a navy background, or rosy-rusts on an extremely dark brown background, with or without a change to a lighter ground within may help you to visualize this design.

Foxgloves appear in #508 Spice of Life (28 x 43).

In this design, be careful to keep a feeling of continuity in the scroll border, by developing all of the sections in a similar manner. One way of using two contrasting colors is to apply one to the veins in the leafy scrolls at ends and sides, and for a dark line of accent and a shaded curling knob in the section between — and use the second hue to shade the remainder of all the sections.

As an example, scrolls of soft grayed green veined and accented in mulberry against an extremely dark dull green outer background and a delicate grayish-green inner background. The iris might be wine with a pink top, the wild roses pink, the rose a deep wine, the fuchsias, purple and rose, and the foxglove creamy white with wine and pink freckles.

PADULAS

Flowers of fantasy! Many of them originated with Great Grandmother, who was never at a loss to cope with any emergency. When creating a design, and confronted with odd spaces to fill, she drew in what was "flower-like." Today we call them "Padulas." Why? Well, that too is fantasy! So, when you find a flower which you or no one else can identify, it must be a Padula! And Padulas are important! When they are small, like these, they provide interesting and colorful details to the edges of floral centers.

Of course their colors should depend upon others you are using in your rug. But as an example, you might use two analogous hues, in (1) (which always reminds me of an oversized hip or haw) like old rose and violet — the violet to outline and accent its curved base and the "puckering" around the top, the deep old rose to fill the base and its lighter tones in the top. A deep reddish purple line at the "waistline" will give a shadow effect. Use a bright yellowish-green for sepals.

Isn't (2) queer? You can use two somewhat contrasting hues

— like tints of Rust in section (B) with dashes of Mummy Brown, and Bronze Green in (A) and (C). It's lovely!

(3) may be adapted to any color, but put a little highlight in, as you would a cherry or grape — with woody-brown for stems.

Let your imagination have wing in (4). Those little eyes at the base of each petal could take on brilliant jewel shades. For instance, Jade, outlined with Maroon with petals of tints of Egyptian Red (which is really a pink).

The bell-shaped flowers may be accented with dark shadows as in (5), and then shaded out into lighter value, especially at the edges. Shadow it on the inside, as shown by shading in sketch. Blend into lighter values at edges of rear petals.

You will often find little dried up stems or branches at the edges of floral bouquets in many of my designs like (6). Keep to the woody-browns, soft faded greens and bronzy tones for them, outlining in light tints (against dark backgrounds) and filling with deeper hues, and vice versa on light backgrounds.

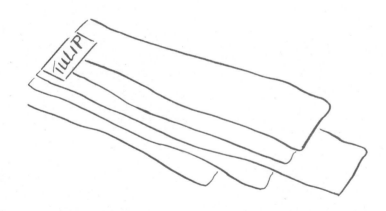

No. 66   Banded Floral

Fanciful flowers — often called padulas — appear in many of my designs, as in #66 Banded Floral (47 x 64½). The main point to remember is to disregard realistic coloring when hooking them. Let your imagination have wing — develop them to fit your color scheme — forgetting reality! You would have to forget reality anyway, because neither you nor I could tell what they were meant to be. These designs are typical of century old rugs, and I've copied them pretty much as they were in some old rug. But they are a delight to hook, for there is no limitation to the colors which you may use.

There are countless small flowers in this pattern, forming a tight floral bouquet and crescent ends for the design.

The border of this design lends interest too.

In this illustration, where a dark toned material has been used for the border against a much lighter background, notice how the edges of the bands have been softened by a lighter value than the background. It may have also been a contrasting color to the band.

Notice the balance of dark and light values in the development of floral detail, borders and background in this design. A good proportion in the use of dark and light values is of great importance to a good color plan.

The subtly mottled inner background does not detract from the floral bouquet because there are no flowers in it of great consequence — all forming a more or less massive effect.

No. 539   Staffordshire Oval

Imagination plays an important part in hooked rugs! If only ruggers would forget reality, and develop their rugs in the colors which will fit into their rooms!

Oftentimes the flowers which appear in some of the designs help to pull them from this realistic world, and some of these flowers are in #539 Staffordshire Oval (60 x 101).

True, the rose appears quite realistic, but try and name the others!

The one who made this rug caught the feeling of fantasy in planning the colors which were keyed to her room — the influence of an excellent teacher! It was almost a monochromatic harmony of rose against a soft gray background. Notice the variance in the use of dark and light values in the flowers, from the darkest in the roses, to the lightest in the smallest flowers — while each of the others takes on an individuality of its own through the manner in which dark values accent its detail.

All of the scrolls are in darker grays than the background and are veined in rose. Their rhythmic flow as they blend from dark to light values give a wispy continuity which pulls all the detail together.

The leaves are so gray a green that they appear almost gray too.

The flower and leaf shades are again brought into the inner "nickel" and the outer "clover" borders.

There are many quaint and almost primitive flowers in some of my designs. Many of them were taken from heirloom rugs. Often they appear in a design which I have restored unchanged. They have their proper place in antique settings where decoration calls for quaint or primitive patterns.

This is the case in #178 Chilcott Cornucopia (33 x 64½). One of the flowers has sharp pointed petals which make me think of a pineapple, while the other has the effect of a sprig of leaves growing upon its petals. The detail is similar to the fanciful flowers seen in crewel work. Perhaps Grandma, in designing her rug, may have been influenced by this type of needlework.

The long scrolly leaves are typical too, and very interesting to develop.

The cornucopia is an intriguing invitation to grade the values of one hue to give a rounding contour to each section through shadowed crevice and highlighted center.

Because these designs come to us from other generations — their colorings too should take on age. So, in hooking them choose the soft faded and muted hues which will make your rug appear very old when finished.

Don't dramatize the detail against extreme contrasts of value in background — but let the design sink away into only slightly lighter or darker values.

FLOWERS OF FANTASY

They came into being with our great grandmothers' day dreaming. These creative, fanciful flowers were her fulfillment of a desire to express herself, though it was through her hook instead of her paint brush. They are another form of padulas, but are often the dominant detail in a design. You must leave the world of reality when you treat them in color.

Use fanciful colors on them — pink and brown blend beautifully, especially if you use Pink and Rust dye. In (1) you could

shadow as indicated by the shading in the illustration in Mummy Brown where the petals crease or lie beneath one another, as shown by (A). Now shade into a delicate milk chocolate brown in part (1), and then into a delicate rusty pink in part (2) of each petal, keeping a half inch away from the base. Use white which has had the faintest tinge of mahogany dye over it to cut the dead white, for the base, and finger it up into the other colors at (B). Use a line of old blue around the center, with a line of dull chartreuse within. Fill the remainder with a brown and gold mixture or plaid material, which will give the effect of tightly packed stamens.

Have you ever made a delicate green flower? This one, which appears in "Dresden Plate," #34, could be a very delicate green, blending into pale yellow and white. Use a subdued orchid for shadows at the base of the petals, as shown by shading. Then blend the delicate green with a chartreuse cast into a delicate yellow at the petal's edge. On some use a creamy white accent, as in (C). On the turned back petals, shade out in the same sequence, using a creamy white accent at irregular places along its jagged petals, as in (D).

Contrasting colors may be used in these queer flowers, especially if you bind them together through a small amount of the proper third color — for example, red and blue bound by purple, which lies between these two in the Color Wheel. In this gloxinia-like fantasy which appears in #339, "Victorian Square," use light old blue for the funnel. Shadow it in a medium purple, as shown by shading (E). Outline the freckles with a deeper purple and fill with fuchsia. At the center opening (F), use dull old gold, outlined with deep purple; then a couple of lines of fuchsia, then one line of a slightly lighter shade of fuchsia, and blend off into a medium purple, like shadows in a funnel. Keep about one-fourth inch away irregularly from the edge, so you can blend this purple into a lighter blue than that used in the funnel. Where the petal's edge lies against the funnel, as in (G), use a whitish-blue edge. Use a brownish-green to outline the base, and shade to a darker center.

Make some of your flowers of fantasy in white, combining it with color accents. In the four-petaled flower marked (4), which appears in SD#5, "Antique," hook one side of the petal white. Hook the center vein and short line of accent in the other side with a light purple, and fill in the remainder of this half with a delicate tint of lavender or pearly gray. Make a crescent of dull green at the base of its center (H). Run a line or two of softer lighter green around the rest of the center, and fill with a very pale, subdued rose.

Now these colors may not interest you at all, in the development of the particular pattern on which you may be working, but they will open up your mind to the possibility of how to approach these queer flowers of fantasy, and where to change color or tone in them. The main thing to strive for is a pleasing harmony in your final result, but remember always, especially in designs which include these fanciful flowers, that neither Nature nor color should limit you. It is of the greatest importance that you achieve an artistic effect in colors that will harmonize in your rug and in your room.

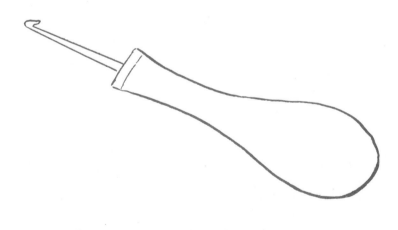

FRUIT

Fruit in design has long been an emblem of plenty. Sometimes it comes spilling out of a cornucopia, and it is used in other ways in the development of a pattern. There are several back issues of the Letter Service dealing with fruit and for an example, I give you one here that covers peaches, plums and cherries.

In a peach, first decide where your blush and highlights are to appear. A lavender mauve blush on the extreme right, as shown by shading in this peach, and of whitish pink for the highlights along the inside curve, as indicated by dashes (A), will give this considerable character. Now between these two extremes, shade soft rose into the blush on curving lines, as in (B). Against the highlight use a salmony-yellow shading into soft peach for most of the cheek. Always swing your lines of hooking with the contour of the peach. In the remaining outside crescent at extreme left, use a soft rose against the highlight and fill to the edge with peach. Don't make the peaches all alike, but you will find that the crescent formed by the creviced side offers an opportunity for highlights. Vary the proportion of blush to that of the general peach tone.

You need about four shades for the plum. In this one a shadow falls upon that part lying next to the overlapping leaf. Use a very dark and quite dull shade of the plum, as shown by shading. Now irregularly finger a slightly lighter but brighter shade of plum into this shadow and around edge, as indicated by curving and irregular lines marked (C). Use your next lighter shade to fill remainder of plum, excepting a patchy highlight (D), in which hook your lightest shade.

The little crescent (E), which appears in most of the cherries, should be an extremely dark shade. In a deep rose red cherry, use dark brown for this accent. Use the darkest shade of your cherry for the shadows, as shown by (F). Pull in two or three loops of a pinkish shade for a highlight (G), and surround it with a line of a little darker tone, using it also at the top of the cherry, after the stem has first been hooked in, as in (H). Fill the remainder of the cherry with a shade slightly lighter, but brighter, than your shadow tone. Each cherry can have its own individuality by the size and position of its highlights, as in (J). Or you can use a crescent shadow to indicate indentation, as in (K).

Of course in all fruit designs, you must again disregard the realistic coloring of any fruit which may be discordant to the colors chosen for the rest of the design. For instance, in a fruit group where there are a few strawberries, but no other similar red detail in the design — and red would not look well with it anyway — by all means make your strawberries greenish white (unripe), with possibly a delicate pink in the cheek and thus save your color plan.

In a set of fruit chair seats, for instance, study the detail in all six designs, (even though they may be slightly different from each other), to be sure that the colors of the various fruits are going to be within your color plan. If there is one that seems to be out of line, use license with your colors and develop it in harmony with the others. Forget reality!

No. 505   ABUNDANCE

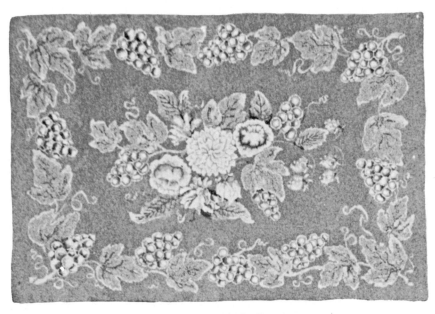

No. 410   SARAH'S BEQUEST

Autumn leaves and fruit make a delightful combination, in #505 Abundance, (32 x 46), and an excellent choice for a dining room or kitchen. Subdue leaves to fruit or vice versa.

Since the fruit occupies the smaller area it is better to use any intensity of color in them, and let your leaves play a secondary part. Yet they may still be somewhat gay! Thus, the purple and red-purples of the grapes may be used for the oak leaves, and for flashing accents in the grape or maple leaves. The red of the apple may be subdued and used for the greater part of the maple leaves — and the rust and pale yellow of the pear may be used for the sumac leaves.

Further repetition may be added by carrying the main color of each leaf over into the next one, as a shadow, vein or accent. Keep the cornucopia in quiet colorings.

Sometimes there are berries and fruit among the flowers, as in #410 Sarah's Bequest, (28 x 41). You need not necessarily make them their true color, if that particular hue does not fit into your scheme. Thus, a strawberry may be a greenish-white, which might repeat or balance similar shades in the grapes at the opposite end.

I am reminded of one of my teachers who built her color plan for this rug around the view from her kitchen window one Spring morning. It held her spell-bound, for she saw the possibility of painting, through her dye pot, the woody-brown earth, the soft varied grays of the stone wall, the delicate greens of spring growth, and the lovely soft reds of the maple buds in the distance.

THE LITTLE THINGS THAT COUNT

In all your detail it's the little things that count!

Little flowers need sharp contrast of values to give the effect of partly opened or curving petals. Try using a very dark value in one petal against a very light value in the next one, and possibly a medium value in a third, etc., as in (1), instead of making them all alike.

A bit of deep color at the very base of the petal, especially in the five-petaled flowers in (2) and (3), will give them more character. Don't be afraid to use blending contrasts, such as purple in a blue flower, or violet in one of rose, or salmon in a yellow flower.

We do not use white often enough in our flowers. True, they should have color accents to give them character. The next time you make small flowers, try white — but tinge them a bit

toward one of your other flowers, by color accents near the center, or, (depending upon the background), at the edge, like (4).

There are many other subtle accents which your own imagination will devise. A tulip, by way of illustration, may have a violet line to accent the center of the petals (5), flanking it on both sides with a grayish-white line. Then go on and make the rest of the tulip mauve, purple, gold, or your desired color.

Don't overlook the unusual effects you can get by strong contrasts of value or hue, especially in morning glories. The funnel, for instance, can be almost white, depending upon the tone of your background, with petals of deep purple at the edge, shading lighter to lavender within, but use a bright rose-red for the curving accents of the petals (6).

If your flower's edge is lost in your background (probably because both are of about the same value), pull in a much lighter or darker shade of the flower at the edge than the value of the background, but not so uniformly that it makes a hard edge.

And flower centers are *so* important — almost as important as a smart, becoming hat, for some of the flower centers do look like little hats perched upon a flower's head. A very simple and effective means of accent is a shadow line of garnet, burgundy, plum or purple, perhaps half way around its base, as in (7).

But if it is a daisy, try a double line of green instead, in a golden center, like (8). Then there are certain mixed goods of gold and black or green and black, which, when hooked, give quite a realistic effect to stamens. These things you will discover as you hook various materials into your flowers, so don't be afraid to try out the strangest looking materials to get the subtle effects that make hooking such fun.

Everyone, I think, likes to make rosebuds. Give that pod a globular or glossy effect by two or three loops of very light green in its center, with perhaps four or five of them in the center of that middle sepal, as suggested in (9), and use plenty of light and dark contrasts on the twisted ends of the sepals which extend out beyond the buds. Just running a very light shade part way along a dark shade will give the effect of turning it over.

Stems are sometimes a problem and must not be too striking. With most, a single line of hooking is all that is required, and in such a case, spot-dyed browns and greens will change that hard effect you get from using a single plain color. If the stem is broad, try a line of light against a line of dark wood-brown, or similarly, two shades of green, but if the stem is very large, like (10), outline both sides of the stem, using a medium tone on one side, and quite an accented highlight along the other side. Or if it is a very bold stem, place your highlights along the middle, which will give it a rounded effect. Don't forget that cut end. Use a darker tone around its contour and fill in with one or two lighter tones.

Tendrils too should be accented. In many cases, because of their single line of hooking, you can use strong color, otherwise they almost disappear when surrounded by background. Sometimes you can accent them a bit by running a second lighter or darker accenting line, as suggested in the dashes of (11). Chartreuse, bright Nile, orange-yellow, greenish-gold, reddish-purple, or even golden brown, are all good for these tendrils.

Then try and see all your flowers as a whole. Does each one stand alone, unrelated to another? Try and make them more friendly. Bring them together through repetition.

The deep wine shade of a rose might be pulled in as a dark accent at the base of a purple tulip —

— the light values of a purple tulip might be used again as a tinge of color mid the light blue edges of a blue morning glory —

— the deeper shades of a blue morning glory might be used as a colorful accent at the base of the petals of a small gray and white flower —

— the shade of one flower may be used as the flower center of another (never mind if they don't grow that way — that is not half as important as UNITY in your rug) —

— a crescent formed from the color of one flower around the flower center of another —

— or perhaps some of the duller shades of a flower may be combined with the leaf hues in developing a sprig of small leaves, thus making them more colorful.

These are all examples of how repetition will bind your floral bouquet together. The eye will be intrigued by the flow of color and the mind delighted with the creative work accomplished.

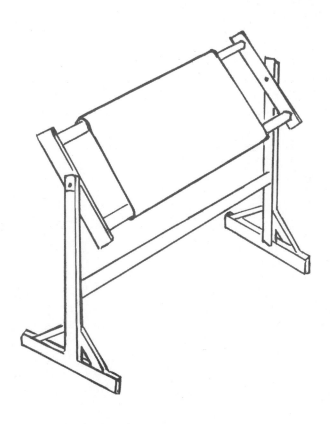

In the older designs, like #214 Gill Antique (31½ x 60¼) you will often find many kinds of flowers growing on the same stem. This seems to be an ear mark of Grandmother's art. The stem from which lilies, roses and morning glories grow in this design serves as a dividing line for two backgrounds. Or, you may carry your outer background to the edge of the twisted ribbon center.

In floral detail of this kind bring your flowers into relationship with each other by repeating the hue of each one as shadows or highlights in others. For instance, the color of your rose and buds (in their tints) might serve as accents in the base of the petals of the lily (the whitish flower), while the light centers of the morning glories may reflect the petals of the lilies in value, even though they may be of another hue.

Whatever is used in the border must be repeated in the center. Though you will find a couple of different flowers at the ends of the floral bouquet, their colors too, should depend somewhat on those used in the outer border. Never use a color in one flower that is not repeated again. Otherwise it will be spotty.

The twisted ribbon border around the floral center is usually developed by contrasting colors, or by contrasting values. Thus, the oval on which the ribbon twists may repeat some hue from the outer detail and be of a contrasting color to the ribbon. Or, you might use a dark value of one hue for the band with medium and light values of the same hue in the ribbon. In this illustration you will notice that this oval band is repeated at the edge of the rug.

No. 507   QUEEN'S DESIRE

#507 Queen's Desire (46 x 80) is shown here in black and white, so that you may compare it with the colored illustration herein of the same pattern — for in the latter I have suggested that you may omit the ribbon border between the floral center and scroll, if desired, without affecting the proportion of the design.

Both rugs illustrated were developed in similar coloring, but with an entirely different effect. In this one, a more dramatic effect was given to the scroll border through "marrying" the deep rose pinks from the flowered center to the greens of the leaves. Thus, in the outer part of the scrolls the deep rose reds have been shaded out to their lighter values at the tips of the scrolls which lie against the outer background, and used only as a veining on the inner part of the scroll which is blended from dark to light soft greens.

There is a feeling of simplicity to the development of all the flowers in one general hue (of many values), and therefore in this case it permits a more dramatic treatment of the scroll.

But when using more than one hue for the floral detail of this pattern, keep the coloring in the scroll as simple as possible, by using but one hue, although it may be of several values. Avoid "painted" scroll effects, or scrolls made of multicolored materials, like plaids and mixtures, lest they confuse both eye and mind.

No. 104   WEDGEWOOD

No. 104B   WEDGEWOOD

Nothing breaks my heart like seeing the background of a design hooked out away beyond the lines I have prepared for you. When you extend it, to possibly take advantage of two or three extra inches of burlap, you throw my proportion out of balance. Usually the scroll or border detail looks out of place against this additional area of background.

It is often, too, that in leaving out details of the design one is conscious that something is missing.

In a few cases where the latter can be done without affecting proportion — as in #507 Queen's Desire, for instance — I have stated this fact.

But if compensation is made for the "operations" you perform — and you do not detract from the design as a whole — there is no reason why you cannot make certain changes to make the pattern more adaptable to your purpose.

#104 Wedgewood ($34\frac{1}{4}$ x $42\frac{1}{2}$) is a case in question. It is a chubby oval. One rugger wanted it a little larger and extended the background to the size desired, making it a rectangle. BUT she made the necessary compensation, repeating the center roses and foliage in the corners to fill these areas, and absorb the extra background.

Because it was pleasing, you may have this design adjusted in this way, as #104B Wedgewood ($37\frac{1}{2}$ x $45\frac{1}{2}$).

Wedgewood makes an excellent companion for #97 Reed Oval.

No. 419   JANE

No. 437   JIMMY

The names of my rugs sometimes take on a very personal note. When my two grandchildren arrived to make my life more interesting, they naturally must have a rug for their room!

So #419 Jane (23 x 36) was made for the little girl I'd always dreamed about, but who didn't arrive until a generation later. Other grandmothers have loved it too!

Its scroll is very simple to develop, and is usually hooked in a gradation of values of one color — though there are many other ways of blending its color. Naturally, its hue must be tied to the center detail in some way, through repetition of color.

It is delightful, when the background under the casual bouquet is shadowed in a manner often seen in old floral paintings.

#437 Jimmy (24 x 36) carries the memory of the day I unrolled the finished rug before his bed. It takes time to design a pattern and transform it to a finished rug, so when it was finished he was big enough to get right down on his knees to smell the rose!

Its leafy scroll lends itself to various blendings of color. In Jimmy's the entire background was a very dark navy. The scroll was made of plaids, dyed to shade from deep old blues into lighter values, but there was enough red in the plaids so that it popped up frequently to give an additional tie-up to the center rose of deep rich red. The foxglove repeated in a more intense blue, the tone of the scroll.

No. 271   LUCY BAKER

Perhaps there is no rug which has come down to posterity that means more to me than #271 Lucy Baker (29 x 63).

One would only have to look at Lucy's rug to visualize the type of person she was, for the design itself, and the wonderful technique she used in hooking it, is evidence of her artistry and meticulous care in performing any task or creative handiwork.

Her granddaughter (then over seventy years) told me about Lucy's life. She was one of those women who was eternally busy. Though she lived a full and active life outside her home, she brought up a fairly large family, and always found time to create beauty through her handwork.

Lucy is always my answer to those who maintain that all old rugs were coarsely hooked. Lucy's rug was nearly a century old, yet its loops were small, low and close. A hundred years of service had only worn them down to appear like a piece of velvet. So hooking seems pretty much the expression of individuals — not of the period in which they lived.

My copy of her rug, which hangs in Rose Cottage, is very much like the original one. Its outer background is an antique black (blackish-green) and has a light center. Its roses are a deep rich red, and the softest maize yellow imaginable (almost a tannish yellow), contrasted with both blue-greens and yellow-greens in the foliage, of a delightful variance of values and intensities. The small "butterfly" scrolls are bronzy-green that blend into a dull brownish-yellow, like the shadows of the yellow roses. Men love it!

LEAVES

Leaves can be VERY interesting! The shading in the following illustrations will indicate where to change from dark to
medium to light values of one color, and suggests various ways
of blending your colors together.

Veins are very important. The right color will give interest
to your leaf — the wrong one may be entirely lost in the tones
of the leaf. Hook them first — either in an extremely light tint
of the color of the leaf, (if you shade the leaf from a dark center
to a light edge), as in (1) — or a contrasting color (to repeat
some flower tone). For instance, in a rug of white roses on a black
background, I used very delicate lavender-whites and palest
pinky-whites for the veins in the varied green leaves. They were
a lovely repetition from the shadows of pink and lavender in
the white roses.

While we think of leaves as green — other hues, especially in their very grayed shades — will often produce a most artistic effect. Thus your gray materials, dyed in weak solutions of Mahogany, Rose, Mummy Brown, Plum, Chartreuse and Mulberry, will open your mind to new ideas.

In (2) where leaves are small, "spot-dyed" materials (where one color runs into another) eliminate shading the leaf in varied values.

In (3) where the vein broadens, exaggerate by dark center vein, flanking on both sides with lighter values of the same hue.

In (4) you can blend several slightly different shades of yellow-green or blue-green — or both of similar values, in the medium area.

In (5) and (6) make the tip turn over by extremely dark or light contrasts on under side, as indicated by shading. Or make this a contrast of hues, such as a light yellow-green on the top side, against a dark blue-green on the under side. In that case, use the same dark shadow of blue-green at the base or along one side, as illustrated.

Rose leaves are almost as fascinating to make as roses; of course you can use a good gradation of one color for them. But spot-dyed materials with a suggestion of reds, purples and blues dyed into blue-greens, or rusty reds and golds dyed into yellow-greens, are best. Then as you cut right through the materials which have been widely spotted, you just naturally shade the color into the development of the leaf. Because of these spots, it is often better to hook the leaf in patchy or mass manner. Use your darkest shades to shadow the base of the leaf, and possibly the veins, part way, as in (A), and then begin to hook your spot-dyed material, working from the shadow out to the edge, which may or may not be highlighted as you wish.

In a group of three rose leaves, the two lower leaves may be slightly darker than the end leaf, for variation. Sometimes it is desirable to greatly exaggerate the tips of rose leaves, as in (B).

There is another delightful development for rose leaves — in fact other types of leaves too — where you develop one side of the leaf in an opposite manner from the other. You vein and shade from extremely dark values of your chosen hue, as in (C), accenting the edge with extreme highlights, as in (D), filling remainder with the intermediate shades. On the opposite side, start with your highlight at the inner edge, irregularly as in (E); shadow the outer edge with darkest shade, as in (F), and bring these two extremes together with your intermediates in the remaining area.

CHRYSANTHEMUM leaves may be quite colorful! No, not bright, but rather soft, subdued rosy-browns, blending into grayish or bronzy-greens. These colors may be a dim reflection from their bright and gay blossoms. With this in mind, give your imagination a little push and then "let it go." It's fun! Use spot-dyed materials, so that when cut straight through, the varied tones will form interesting blotches of color and give them char-

acter. But first put in the veins — a very dark blackish-green.
Hook in your highlights (your lightest shade) where the light
might fall upon the leaf, or where it curls, as suggested by (A).
Hook irregular shadows along the center vein, or where the curled
edge throws a shadow, as in (B), remembering that a dark shadow
next to a highlight accents each more. Now use your intermediate tones to bind these two extremes together. A little dull accent
of the flower color here and there, along one side of a "mum"
leaf, as in (C), supplies a subtle accent.

POPPY leaves usually run toward the blue-greens or gray-
greens. Use highlights to form bulges, and where the leaf curls
over, as in (D), and then shade back gradually to a dark center
around the vein. Don't make all your leaves alike — place the
highlights in various ways, sometimes having the entire tip of
the leaf quite light. Keep in mind when making leaves that you
seldom see them FLAT — they usually curl or curve and drop
with grace, complementing their blossoms. With this in mind
you're going to be amazed at your own creative ingenuity!

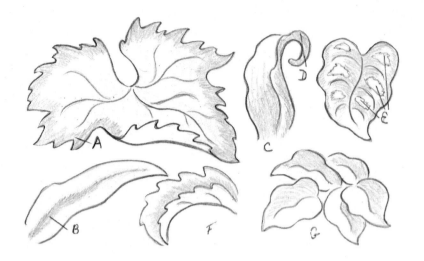

GRAPE leaves may be very colorful! Greens spot-dyed with purple or blue are very effective. Where the leaves demand attention, they could be broadly edged with accenting color, as in (A).

Lily leaves may have a very broad dark center of the leaf color, as in (B).

If a tulip leaf curls back or over, as in (C), use dark values, as indicated by dark shading. Make the edge which curls over, (D), a brighter shade of your leaf color. Then fill in the rest of the turn-back with a dark value — dark enough to make quite a contrast to the lighter shades of the face of the leaf.

Make your morning glory leaves BULGE by the use of highlights, as in (E). Use dark shadow tones near the center vein and all along the outer edge, and then use medium values to bind the two extremes together.

Where a leaf curls, as in (F), give it a little "oomph" with a contrasting color, such as a grayed pinkish-lavender on the underneath side of the leaf, deepening it at the lower edge. Use deep blue-greens on the top side of the leaf along the center, shading lighter near the edges.

When a group of leaves lap over each other, make each more distinctive by shading one side of each leaf light, the other side dark, as in (G). Or use two analogous colors, such as yellow-green on one side, blue-green on the other.

No. 338   Hills Leaves

No. 485   Winter Bloom

Leaves lend themselves beautifully to all sorts of designs — in borders framing the main detail — scattered carelessly — or set into repeat diamonds or squares.

The rule of repetition applies in all such patterns. Whatever the hue of one leaf in a diamond or square — repeat something of it — as a shadow or highlight — in the hues of another — so that the eye follows from one to another.

If there are bands or borders in the design, develop them of some of the hues within the leaves — or some dark value of one hue which may be dominant in your color plan.

They need not be realistic in coloring. Again, the important question is, "Where are you going to use the rug, and what colors are dominant there?" Then let fancy take over!

Sometimes it is the simplicity of a design that gives it great charm. I think that is true of #338 Hills Leaves (30½ x 52).

Simplicity of coloring will add to its charm. It can be outstanding among others.

In a design of this type, where the leaves are over-sized and not too realistic, be imaginative in planning its colors.

One of this design at Rose Cottage has two slightly different light grayish homespun blankets for backgrounds, the lighter on the inside. The largest leaves are shaded in deep wines to lighter soft mulberry, with veins and accents of medium old blue. The second group is reversed, being of medium old blue with veins and accents of light wine and soft mulberry. The inner leaves are pale dull chartreuse yellow, with veins and accents of light old blue. Thus, each group repeats something of the hue of another. All three hues are used together in the inner band.

The begonia and coleus leaves that form the repeat pattern of #485 Winter Bloom (30 x 50½) may be as colorful as you wish. One that I always loved was in purplish red begonia leaves and chartreuse green coleus leaves against a creamy homespun background. The softer and duller shades of the same hues were blended to frame the diamonds. A light background may be carried through the whole rug, if desired, but in such a case a few lines of color (usually something used in the diamond border) should be repeated at the edge.

A combination of leaves and scrolls like #489 Maple Rhythm (30 x 59) is an interesting pattern to hook. Maple leaves lend themselves beautifully to the fall colorings — all of which — in their softer and more subtle shades — may be repeated in the scroll within. But let the leaves dominate — the scrolls being secondary.

Dark values are hooked at the base or near the center part of leaf around the main rib.

One which is vivid in my memory had a dark woody brown background with an inner background which had been spot dyed a light brownish-cream, so that as you cut through the material a delightful variation was formed in its tones.

Some of the maple leaves were shaded from green to soft gold — others from brownish-gold into light green — and still others from dull soft red into light gold, all veined in a gradation of greens. The scrolls were of the soft golds with green veins with delicate green accents in the tips of the curls of the scroll and the turn of the knob. But they were all subordinate to the leaves, the important detail of the design.

The leaves in this design are bold enough to be treated in a modern manner through the proper colors. When well chosen they may be closely allied to the color scheme of a room. Can you visualize it in grayed-coral leaves and scrolls with chartreuse veins, treated flat with no shadows, upon a two toned gray background?

Various types of ferns and berries form a delightful design in #393 Ferns (47¼ x 96). I picked all kinds of ferns from the woods around my camp for this pattern. Give each fern an individual development of color.

They have been repeated and placed in such a manner that the problem of balance has been eliminated if you repeat each particular one in the same colors wherever it may appear.

Notice how the dark values are carried three-fourths of the way along some of the longer fern fronds, then shaded into small areas of medium values and thence into tips of still lighter value. Naturally the values in one type of fern should not differ too much from others, although their hues may differ — but if one is quite dark and another extremely light you will interrupt the all-over border effect so necessary in this design.

My "Ferns" at Rose Cottage is such a livable rug — one never tires of it. Seal brown dye was used over tan to get a medium woody brown background under the ferns, with a slightly lighter shade in the inside background. Each spray of ferns is treated with individuality in blue-greens, gray-greens, yellow-greens and even purplish blue-greens (spot-dyed of course) with dull reddish sumac, and berries.

Another lovely "Fern" made by one of my teachers in Michigan is a harmony of reseda greens and rust and warm browns and chartreuse berries against a warm mahogany background.

REED OVAL

No. 97

The shape of a rug is often important. Thus, besides the rectangles, there are designs in ovals, rounds and squares. In using them, consideration should be given to the space to be filled, and to any other rugs used within the room.

Don't you think the oval has more appeal if but one is used without competition within a room? Perhaps an exception is the use of a pair of large ovals to flank both sides of a larger room sized rug, in a very large room.

In the average size, an oval is pleasing if placed parallel with a bed or before an extremely wide chest of drawers. Never use one "kitty-corner."

#97 Reed Oval (33 x 60¼) makes a pleasing bedroom rug.

The small padulas and tendrils in the center bouquet and flowered border are fun to hook.

The background may be the same shade throughout or changed along the twisting branches of the border, from a dark value outside to a lighter one within, as in this illustration.

Naturally the flowers and buds in the border should be of the same colors and shades as those in the center.

This design has often been used by mothers for the hope chest of a daughter. Once one was made of materials full of sentiment, including an old creamy homespun blanket for the center background. The rug was finished just before the date of the daughter's wedding, so a little of her travelling suit was hooked into one of the flowers. How precious!

No. 391   Autumn

A fat chubby oval often fills your need for a rug to be placed in an area of unusual dimensions, which are not often found in a rectangle design. These areas sometimes appear in a room where dominant flower and scroll designs and many other types of design are not fitting.

In #391 Autumn (48 x 55) discretion in the use of scroll, leaf and flower detail has produced one of great charm.

It has the feeling of antiquity! Its simple boat-like scrolls, overlapping leaves, wreath of leaves with berries, and central nosegay of roses and fuchsias seem to express a fine feeling of restraint in the one who designed it long, long ago. For it was copied from a precious heirloom.

In this illustration, the outer background was a very dark brown with soft bronzy-gold scrolls. The overlapping leaves shade from brownish-reds into rust and soft goldish tips, and are veined with greens. The wreath was green with bittersweet berries. The bouquet included brownish-red and bronzy-gold roses and the fuchsias repeated the bittersweet shades of the berries. Thus, you will notice that all the hues in the outer detail have been repeated in the center. Mixtured materials that give a "flecky" effect to a background, as shown in the middle area here, will lend interest to a pattern in which there is a large background area.

No. PP9   Round Beauty

No. 416   Floral Roundlet

Round rugs have their place. In a room with the proper space they form a throne-like area for the chair before the dressing table.

PP#9 Round Beauty (40 x 40) is full of interesting and varied detail. One of the flower hues is carried over into the small blossoms which crop out between every other scroll, and the small sprig of leaves in the alternating spaces repeat the green of the foliage. The greens of your foliage are always a safe color for the scroll.

Well I remember the day this rug was made! The pupil said: "I simply haven't enough of any one thing to make my inner background!" From her bag we pulled three small bundles of materials in slightly different tones, but enough alike so that when fingered together carefully, the darker values shadowed the inner edge of the scrolls, and blended gradually into the lighter shades in the area beneath the floral center. It is the utilization of materials "as is"—when applied artistically—that brings the greatest thrill to the rugger!

#416 Floral Roundlet (37 x 37) is a dainty and airy design, very appropriate for a young girl's dressing table. Draperies or bedspread colors may be used for flower and leaf hues and the blending of the scroll. Perhaps the light background might be a reflection of the general shade of the dressing table skirt or the tone of the walls.

No. 432   RING AROUND THE ROSEY

No. 125   GRAY'S CIRCLE

It is always interesting to compare dark and medium backgrounds. Sometimes it helps you to decide the effect you want.

In #432, Ring Around the Rosey (37 x 37), the flowers will appear more striking when played against an extremely dark or black background.

The twisted ribbons, which form a ring around the flowers, should both be of the same hue, though the ribbons may shade slightly darker where they weave under and lighter where they cross over, but these ribbons were not planned for two hues.

An entirely different effect would be achieved if the background was light and the ribbons a flower hue from within.

A still different effect would be secured if color was used in the outer background with a pleasing contrasting color in the ribbons, both of which of course should be closely related to the hues of the floral or leaf details.

A medium background has the tendency of absorbing or permitting your colors to melt away into the background, as shown here in #125 Gray's Circle (47 x 47).

In a design like this where there is a great variety of flowers, and especially where one flower may not appear again, watch out for balance! Use the hue of such a single flower in that of another kind. White is always safe to use where variety of flowers may call for many hues, providing it is repeated enough so it does not appear spotty. Watch out that only one color is in full intensity — and let the others follow.

FUNDAMENTALS OF SCROLLS

Scrolls! Is there anything more typical of our Early American hooked rugs than the scroll designs?

These scrolls have a marked individuality. Even when simple in design, clever blending and contrast of colors will transform them into a lovely decoration.

All scrolls in the old rugs are not necessarily good — some being quite crude or angular — yet even they have sometimes been redeemed by Time's toll of softened lines and faded colors.

Generally speaking, scrolls can be divided into four classes:

(1) Those which form a simple, unobtrusive frame for a floral picture,

(2) Those which dominate the whole pattern, causing the usually simple center to be of secondary importance,

(3) Those which have a fairly even balance between scroll and floral center,

(4) Those of miscellaneous character, sometimes cropping out from flower or leaf, but usually of small repetitive type forming a more or less conventional border or outline.

All of these may also be classified as:

(a)   Filler scrolls
(b)   Leafy scrolls
(c)   Feather scrolls
(d)   Knobby scrolls

CLASS 1.

The main thing to bear in mind is that the floral center is the "picture"— the scroll serving as its frame. Therefore, the scroll is secondary in importance — merely supporting or complementing the picture within. When finished, this scroll should blend into the background, throwing the point of interest to the center of the rug. However, in spite of its secondary role, bright colors — yes, even vivid shades *used sparingly,* are sometimes needed —

and properly used — will blend into just the right touch or sparkle to give the scroll character.

Contrasts between the background and scroll — that is, a dark or vivid scroll on a light background, or an extremely light or brilliant scroll on a dark background, should be avoided in this simple type of scroll, for this would throw the scroll into sharp relief, and draw attention from the real point of interest.

Because of their intricacy of design and coloring, probably the simplest material to use in these scrolls is plaids, mixtures or checks. When cut and hooked, the design of the material has been dissipated but the somewhat uneven effect and the peculiar coloring when the various colored threads are brought together with the hook are delightful to the eye. The general tone of the material when hooked, will give the key to the right color to be used for accentuating vein and outline. But here again, consideration must always be given to the background and the colors to be used in the center to keep a good relation between all three.

Dyed material is an excellent medium for scrolls of this type, especially when there is either a wide variance in the tones, or a spot-dyed material is used.

Solid shades should be used with great care in scrolls of this type, and only when the shades are soft or subdued enough to sink well into the background.

Of course the treasured material, when it comes to scrolls of this kind, is paisley, for its myriad hues so delicately woven together, when hooked, give the scroll a delightful soft coloring which nothing else can duplicate. Variety and interest too can be brought into the paisley scroll, when several different kinds are used. If you haven't too much of one kind, mix your different paisleys from the very beginning. #297, "Newhall Scroll," is a good example of this type of "filler" scroll.

You use a contrasting color in the veins of a filler scroll — if it has veins — and edge the scroll with the same hue or a lighter or darker shade of it, depending upon your background.

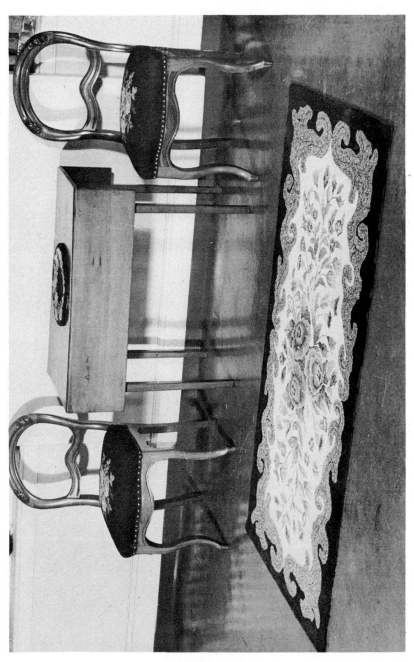

No. 297   Newhall Scroll

In #297, Newhall Scroll (31½ x 71½) — the whole color plan started with a treasured paisley shawl. The scroll was veined with dark greenish-blue and edged with turquoise blue. The dark rich red paisley was used as a filler which melted into the outer black background.

The floral detail was harmonized to the paisley shades. The center roses were shaded from the paisley reds to reddish-salmon highlights. The smaller flowers were turquoise blue and lavender, and the foliage was in varied blue-greens.

It is shown here with a pair of needlepoint chairs and an antique table with which it is used.

But if you don't happen to have one of these lovely old shawls, some plaids make good substitutes for paisley. Mellow the plaids somewhat in a weak solution of dye. If they tend toward red and green with whitish squares, try a very weak Peacock solution — only enough to mellow the red, soften the green and tint the lighter part.

Sometimes a medley of plaids will give a delightful effect. You will never know until you try these mixed materials or colors what will happen as you hook them to the surface of your burlap — but that's all part of the fun!

Because the roses are large, avoid brilliant colors. Either use extremely soft shades if they are to be in medium hues — or use a number of very dark shades with a small amount of bright accents if your roses are to be deep. If light roses are preferred, use more of the medium soft shades and a smaller amount of bright hues. Then accent with delicately tinted highlights.

However, as stated before, don't dramatize this type of scroll. Keep it quiet, so it will melt away into the background.

CLASS 2.

In the dominating scroll, however, the rules are just reversed. The scroll has such a definite character that rich colors may be brought into play within its lines. The eye is attracted and the interest held by the intricacy of its blending. The veins, made prominent by contrasting or complementary color, become an interesting detail. The body of the scroll should be carefully blended and the outline be a contrasting value to the background. The center is noted for its simplicity, and repeats in a "me too" manner some of the less dominating colors in the scroll.

When there is a difference in the detail of one part of the design from another — like the following illustration — there is an opportunity to slide into lighter or darker values, or neighboring hues — but always keep a feeling of continuity by repeating some of the hues from the previous detail. This rug is shown on page 162.

Can't you see how lovely this design might be if each scroll were developed slightly differently so they would vary somewhat, and yet, through balancing, achieve an unusual effect?

A leafy scroll is apt to be a dominating feature of a design.

In this type of scroll the leaf spreads out in undulating lines from its central and rather excessive side veins. Accent the four main veins by dark and rich lines and flank them, as shown by

(B), with a medium and softer shade of the same hue. Then follow the veins with the dark shades of your desired color of the scroll. Being such large scrolls, keep them somewhat soft and grayed — always swinging your line of hooking with the curve of the veins (in C), and avoid carrying these dark shades much beyond the middle of the scroll — then use slightly lighter shades when veins converge, flaring the shades out toward edge. Then, with the lightest, edge and finger back into these flared lines. Now you can get some delightful effects if you dare to blend your analogous hues. For instance your scroll might start off in varied greens, but as you approach the four extremities, the first might shade out into a blue-green tip, the second toward a yellow-green, the top tip toward a very soft grayed bronze, and the one on the left hand side might shade from the green base into blue-green and thence into a grayed blue tip.

The scroll in #191 Chilcott Leaves (36 x 68½) is shaded from a very dark value where scroll begins, to extremely light highlights where it ends. This wide variation of values is very necessary in this plume-like scroll if you are to avoid a flat appearance. This same variance of value is stressed, in this illustration, by the shadows of the leaves interrupting the scrolls and in the center foliage.

Since this scroll covers a large area, the intensity of color used in it must not be too bright, except possibly in its rich dark shadows or as accent in bright light tips, to give it character.

In my rug of this design, the scrolls were blended in soft greens, or grayed mulberry, with leaves of blue-greens. The green scrolls were veined with deep mulberry at the base shading into soft mauve pinks at the tips, and the mulberry scrolls are veined with the greens. The mulberry scrolls are reflected in the roses in the center bouquet. The center foliage repeats the varied blue-greens from the border detail.

In a dominating scroll of this type, one can give the design a modern effect by omitting the flowered detail and using modern color. Thus, a delightfully fresh development of this design was one in which the large plume-like scrolls at the end shaded from a deep dull coral red, blending out into extremely light grayish-coral tips, veined in a gradation of grays. The leafy detail interrupting the scroll was a warm gradation of grays, veined in the varied corals. The outer background was a very dark and dull blue-green, with a plain slightly lighter inner background of a spot-dyed blue-green mottled in a subtle manner.

No. 542   GODDESS OF FORTUNA

#542 Goddess of Fortuna (45¾ x 95¾) has all the ear marks of the dominating scroll. Its cornucopia of flowers and sprays of small leaves are of minor importance in its color plan, and serve only as a colorful accent to the rest of the detail in this pattern.

The rug illustrated is most dramatic!

Its background is a somewhat rich and very dark brown.

Its scrolls are also in browns, shading from a deep rich golden brown at the base of the cornucopia into gradually lighter values, and turning at its extremities into a rich cream. In some of them yellow, soft pinks or pinky-lavenders have been fingered into the cream, to give each one quite a tinge of that particular color.

Their veins of blue-greens, which shade out into delicate turquoise in the lightest tips, reflect the general shading of the cornucopia which changes from a deep dark blue-green crevice to a light grayed green scallop and flaring top.

The rich brownish-reds of the roses, which are used again as heavy accents in the base of the tulips shading out to lighter values at the top, are repeated in duller hues in the long sprays of small leaves in the opposite corners.

Naturally this rug — especially in these colorings — must be the whole show in any setting. It will stand no competition!

Don't use any striking contrast between outer and inner background of this rug, lest you wind up with a light squarish effect in the middle which will detract from the design as a whole.

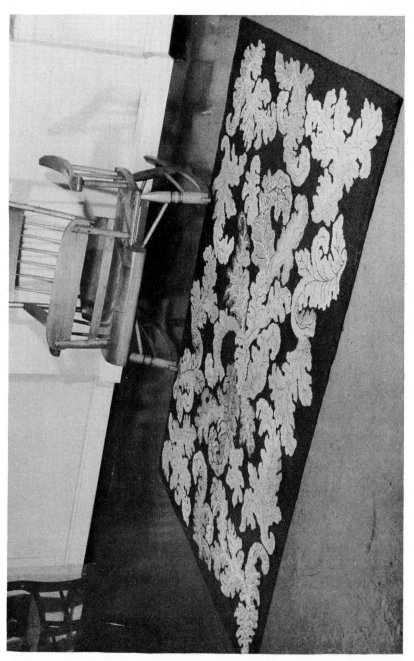

No. 446   Sylvan Scrolls

#446 Sylvan Scrolls (54 x 88) is a good example of a leafy scroll. These quaint scrolls — the imagination of some dear soul of long ago — offer boundless opportunities in color development. In this one, the scrolls are treated in a flat manner, and shaded in warm hues — some starting with soft dull reds, blending into weak golds and light tanny-yellows, with green veins — others in grayish greens blending into brownish-golds and weak reds, with red veins — while still others are golden browns shading into soft golds and weak red tips with green veins — all on an extremely dark background. Note how exaggerated some of the veins appear. The whole effect is quaint and the color plan suggests beautiful fall foliage.

When I look at this rug I am always reminded of the pupil who made it. She lived on a farm in Wisconsin and had always wanted to travel. She sold her rug, depositing the funds in the Savings Bank. This paid all her expenses to our Exhibit in Worcester the following year, when twenty-seven other pupils and their teacher chartered a bus for the trip!

This is the type of design in which you can utilize a variety of scarce materials — but oh, I pray, not in a hodge podge manner! Plan it carefully! Put all your materials in separate piles of each general hue. Now choose those which will combine and create harmony. It does not matter that you have only a little of this and much more of that. Use the first sparingly and scatter it throughout the rug; use a more generous amount of the latter at frequent intervals.

You can give these scrolls a plumy effect by using dark shades near the veining, flaring them out and fingering medium shades down into them, and then working out to lighter edges if preferred. Use closely related colors, so that the effect will not be spotty.

CLASS 3.

A good example of this class is one showing a fairly even balance between a feather scroll and floral center.

In this type of scroll you should have a contrasting hue in the veins — deep enough so that when the scroll colors are worked against it, it will not be lost. Let it fluctuate and deepen in the roll of the corners — and lighten it as it grows near the tips.

Deep or dark colors may be used with great success in these feathery scrolls, but avoid the flat appearance of several lines of one shade. Instead, carry your lines of a single color or tone through from base to near the tip, and shade gradually into lighter values, as shown here.

In all the scrolls of Class 3 there should be a close and intimate relationship between the scroll and floral center. One way to achieve this is by repeating in the scroll some of the floral or leaf colors.

The leaf colors are safer unless you use extremely dull (grayed) floral shades.

The knobby scrolls often come in this class, and the curls usually grow lighter until they reach their highlight in the knob of the scroll — as shown by shading in the following illustration.

CLASS 4.

This type is usually a repeated or reversed scroll, to form a more or less conventional border. It is therefore necessary to keep a feeling of continuity through flowing lines. Thus each scroll might be developed the same, gradually shading from dark values to light values of one hue, or with dark and light accents as shown by this illustration.

Because they are a frame for the center, keep the hues soft. Avoid brilliant or harsh colors which would demand attention!

Or you can combine two hues in a scroll of this kind — but in doing so be sure that the two hues balance in values or strength of color where the two colors meet, so they will slide together, without too sharp breaks. It is done easiest by using analogous hues; thus blue flows into green — green into gold, etc. The scroll becomes even more interesting if you shade from a dark value to one of the hues into light values of the second — thus deep blue shading into light green, or deep green into light gold.

Then in this miscellaneous group, there is the fanciful or imaginative scroll which crops out from leaf or flower, disappears and turns up again in unexpected places, as in "Antique," #5.

Be careful of sharp breaks between the color of the scroll and that of preceding leaves. Avoid extremely contrasting colors to those of the nearby leaves. Analogous hues are best. Squint your eyes and if the scroll stands out stronger than the nearby leaf — (or vice versa) — then you have failed to make your colors flow together.

It is not my intention to limit you to any set color combinations for any design. I would not rob you of the joy of creating. But my suggestions of certain colorings should awaken your own imagination. Let it have wing! True, in practice, some of your ideas may have to be changed. But don't hesitate to try, even if you have to pull out color. If it doesn't give you the desired effect, try something else. Time spent in pulling in one color against another, watching its effect upon surrounding shades, is time well spent, and gradually you will build up a fund of knowledge on color which will be of great value in the future — not only in your rugs, but in everything about you.

Even the trials and tribulations you may have in developing your scrolls will fade in memory, as you recall with pleasure how you took the color out of this material, dyed it into that one, and had to resort to some choice old bits of wool from Grandmother's trunk before you secured the effect you were after. Oh, they are a heap of fun — these scrolls!

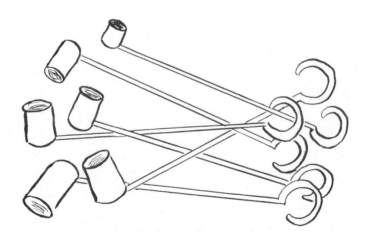

Notice the variance in the two corners of SD5 Antique (32 x 60) yet they balance beautifully. These diagonally balanced corners are typical of the Early American rugs. Here is your cropping scroll, which appears from under flower or leaf detail to give continuity to the design. If you use analogous hues in leaf and scroll your colors will flow together, and you will not be conscious of where leaf ends and scroll begins. Thus, blue-green leaves will flow into yellow-green scrolls.

I have one at Rose Cottage which has a black outer background made from an old shawl, giving it a dull antique appearance. (New black is inclined to have a sheen.)

Mine looks much like this illustration, because of its inner light background made from an old grayish-white homespun blanket. The roses in the corners are a deep rose-pink — the peony a light pink with pinkish-white edges — and the daisies are a grayish-white. In the opposite corners the 4 petalled padula (of which you'll read more about later on) is a very light grayish lavender with white accents. The same hues are carried into the center bouquet, with the addition of a light greenish-blue and very grayed orchid in the smaller flowers.

I recall with great pleasure the artistic effect achieved in this design by a Southern pupil. She dyed no materials, and depended entirely upon soft grayed pinks, dull reds, old blues, dull lavenders, gray and sagey-greens — all from her treasure of stored materials — and played them against a medium gray outer background and a slightly lighter inner gray background. She was an artist! Her rug had the mellow tone of one which might have been a century old!

No. 388   Holway Gem

No. SD1   Ruby

Another cropping scroll appears in #388 Holway Gem (26 x 45) and because it runs along only the long sides of the pattern — plan well! Its hue should be a neighbor (on the color wheel) of that long leaf which precedes it, so that the colors will "flow" together and give continuity to the border. Otherwise, especially if you use contrasting hues, the scroll will appear to stand alone when the rug is completed.

It is an unimportant part of your pattern anyway, merely serving as a division line for two backgrounds — so keep it quiet.

Dark shades hooked along the inner lines of the repeating boat-like scrolls in SD1 Ruby (29¾ x 42½) — and highlights along the outer edges — give continuity to the border.

Notice how the background has been lightened under the floral center, like a sunburst. Care must be taken to finger the lighter shades irregularly into the others where they join so there will be no sharp break between the two.

One of this design at Rose Cottage is a favorite of mine, because the teacher who made it was so clever in utilizing turkey red material — some of which was dyed a very dark red for an outer background. The color was then stripped from other turkey red which resulted in a pale pinkish-white. Part of it was then dyed in an extremely delicate tint of Seal Brown which provided a pinky-beige inner background. The rest was dyed several deep rich reds shading up to a medium reddish-rose for the carnations and roses — tints of the reds for the remaining flowers — and yellow-greens for scrolls and leaves.

A feather scroll, which divides attention with the floral bouquet, is shown in #351 Penny Scroll (34 x 61½). This one shades from a dark mulberry knobby end into lighter mauve curls which are highlighted on the upper side of the curls with grayish mauve-pink and delicate gray (almost white). They lie against a medium light gray background.

The mulberry and mauve of the scrolls are repeated in most of the flowers in the bouquet center, and the foliage is of soft blue-greens. The grayish-white of the scrolls is accented by the small white flowers with colorful accents at their centers.

The background under the band and "pennies" is a deep grayed shade of mulberry, and the band and pennies are the grays of the inner background.

Sometimes in the development of this pattern the outer background is brought in to meet the scroll, but this forms an irregular effect which to me is not quite as pleasing as this illustration.

A word of warning about the pennies! Be careful of sharp bright colors or values which will make them stand out strongly against the background. Instead, use a dyed material which fluctuates in each penny. Or — make each penny of one of three differing values of a color. Or — make each penny of one of three neighboring hues all of about the same value. This provides a variance of value of one hue in *each* penny, or a variance of value in every three pennies, or a variance in the hue of every three pennies. For instance, depending somewhat on your background — the pennies might reflect the leaf colors — one penny being slightly yellow-green, another green, and another slightly blue-green. In such a case you could shade the three greens into the narrow band border.

No. 546   Elite

A knobby scroll is food for imagination! In #546 Elite (36 x 72) the little knobs offer an opportunity to blend out into extreme highlights of the same color or a neighboring hue (if it has some relationship to the rest of your rug).

In this rug, however, the outside background appeared to be a dark reddish brown, with an inner background of warm cream. The scrolls were shaded in soft golden browns blending into dull golds and soft yellow accents in the edges of the knobs. Notice the variance in the development of the curls of the scrolls, some all of similar values, while others are highlighted on one side.

The floral center was dramatized by using the dark outside background beneath the bouquet. This is rather tricky to do, because it should not be too apparent to the eye. Sometimes the detail does not offer a breaking point between the shadow and the center background. In this case, it provides a good foil for the luscious coral pink rose, brownish-gold tulip and purplish-blue morning glories which dominate the center. The surrounding pansies, and those grouped at the two ends of the rug, repeat in softer tones the colors of the three main flowers. The leaves run to the yellow-greens and gray-greens, and are developed in a simple manner so that they merely emphasize the beauty of the floral detail.

If preferred, the outside background may be brought into the section under the pansy ends, leaving a light oval inner background. Or you can use three shades, subtly different in value, in these three areas. Or the entire background may be one shade.

No. 500   Season's Promise

No. 475   Inspiration

Sometimes a scroll will spread out in broad leafy fashion to form a frame for a floral bouquet, as in #500 Season's Promise (28 x 46).

Because of its large area its color must not be too bright. The veins play an important part in the scroll — and may sometimes be flanked with lighter values of its hue. They should always shade gradually lighter at extremities if the tips of the scroll are lightened.

The scroll may be shaded darker along the inner side of the vein, including the knobs at ends and sides — or darker only at the beginning of the knob at the center sides and grow gradually lighter at the ends.

Spot-dyed materials work out beautifully in this scroll when they are dyed in three values — the first piece in dark values, the second piece in medium values, and the third in tints to form light values for the edges or knobs.

Tulips are fascinating to hook. Be careful of the long tulip leaves on a light inner background. Avoid extremely dark values or they may appear hard when finished.

A scroll may be extremely slender too — and ofttimes mingles with leaf and flower, as in #475 Inspiration (23 x 36). Because it is interrupted by floral detail, it is best to develop it in a color which will flow into the sur-rounding hues.

In this illustration, the blue-greens in the scrolls help to maintain a certain individuality, yet they flow into the yellow-greens of the foliage. The vein repeats the mauve of the roses.

"Inspiration" is a delightful choice for a young girl's room.

Somewhere between the leafy and knobby scrolls, there is a type which includes both of them, which I refer to as a meandering scroll, and #378 Lady Bountiful (34 x 71) is a typical example. It meanders gracefully around the border, with roses and foliage cropping out here and there. Naturally they interrupt the continuity of the scroll, and this is something to keep in mind when you develop it in color. The more contrast there is between the hues of scroll and roses — the greater the interruption — and since continuity is an important point in the development of a border, give it consideration when planning your colors.

Therefore, this design might cause you some limitation in the use of color. For instance, I can visualize this rug in soft green scrolls against a dark brown background, with the rose leaves of darker greens, and the roses in soft yellows blending into yellow-green shadows. The greens and yellows being analogous, would flow together.

But if you choose a blue-green scroll and a bright red rose you will arrive at a very spotty effect because they are complementary contrasts.

Naturally the clusters of grapes at each end must be in harmonious color to the rest of your color plan, even though you have to draw upon your imagination.

Every design to me is like a book, to remind me of various rugs made from them. This one brings to mind a lovely rug (made by a teacher in Minnesota) which had an outside background of a soft greenish-blue tweed. It came from an old coat for which she had paid only fifteen cents at a rummage sale. Isn't it wonderful to transform useless materials into rugs of beauty!

No. 398   OLLIVIA

A knobby scroll with a delightful open floral center is illustrated in #398 Ollivia (48 x 88). The scrolls are treated in a somewhat flat manner, with only suggestive shadows in the four corners. The lighter and soft greens of the foliage in the center were used for the scrolls, with veining of a gradation of the deep rose-reds of the main flowers. The floral center was almost monochromatic — each of the different kinds of flowers being developed in varied shades of the rose-reds, some ranging up into very light pinks. Yet, other colors were used for small shadows and emphasis, especially in the tulips.

This design is available with the scrolls spread — not quite meeting at ends and sides, in a larger size (#398A, 55 x 96). In this case you are limited to the same background all the way to the edge of the rug. If using a light background I suggest you shade it darker in the last five rows at the edge, or repeat four or five lines of color from the center — preferably your grayer shades of leaf greens.

I am always impressed with the ambition and willingness of some ruggers to change certain details of a rug when they do not entirely satisfy them — especially long after a rug is finished and in use. I have in mind a teacher who had used this design with spread scrolls against a light background, for her bedroom. Later she made some rugs with a dark wine outer background for the same room, and wishing to bring the rugs into closer relationship, she ripped out all the outer background on her Ollivia. I extended the scroll to meet at ends and sides, and she hooked in the dark wine background to bind it to the other rugs more closely.

No. 484   First and Second Fiddle

No. 413   Garden Memories

In planning a rug which has two sets of scrolls, make the smaller one of secondary importance in color. This plan is suggested by the name of #484 First and Second Fiddle (28 x 46).

The inner scrolls if smaller may be lighter than the outer group or they may be of a weaker intensity of color.

The division line in backgrounds may be as shown in this illustration, or the inner scrolls may lie upon the lighter background.

One rug I shall always remember had a dark brown outer background which was repeated within the inner scroll, thus dramatizing the soft gold and yellow flowers in the center, while the intermediate background between the scrolls was a soft medium beige. Both backgrounds were a wonderful foil for the varied greens used in the two sets of scrolls.

Twin scrolls also offer an opportunity for three backgrounds. They may be three values of one hue — or a pleasing contrasting color may be used in the intermediate area.

In #413 Garden Memories (23 x 39) the center may be bound to the border by repeating the pansy colors in the exaggerated veins of the graceful scrolls. Or repetition within the center may come through binding the delicate greens of the ferns to the shadows of the lilies of the valley. Or, if chartreuse greens are used to accentuate the contour of the ferns, use it again as whiskers, or edges to a white pansy, and thus make a double tie-up to the white lilies of the valley.

BORDERS

Borders make simple and interesting frames in the design of a rug.

In a straight lined border, like simple parallel lines, as in (A), they may be a contrast of value to the background, like a tan to creamy band on a dark brown background. Or they may be a contrasting hue, like a blue-green band on a brown background.

Of course the more contrast there is between the value of your background and that of the border, the more striking the effect. This is sometimes desirable, and sometimes something to avoid. If using a dark border against a light background, slightly lighten the edge of the border to avoid a hard line at the edge of the band. If the bands are broad, graduate the shades from very light edge to medium center if on dark background, or a medium edge to a dark center if on a light background.

Naturally the border should have some relationship to the center detail. It might repeat the leaf shades — or in softer and more subtle shades reflect the dominant floral detail.

Paisley is ofttimes used as a filler for these bands, with a soft contrasting hue to outline the edges.

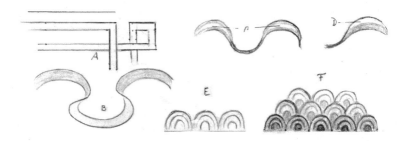

Ribbon borders may be made to turn over by using a contrasting dark value of the same hue, darkest where shaded, as in

(B). Or they may shade to a darker value where they narrow, with highlights where they broaden, as in (C). Or you can shade the ribbon darker in the narrow part and at the base of the broad part, and place your highlight at the edge of the latter, as in (D).

Sometimes the border will be in a single row of shells, like (E), or in a series like (F). Again the colors to be used should be a repetition of something from the center. In (E) you can cleverly introduce single lines of contrasting hues in its development — thus both floral and leaf hues may be used. Analogous hues will slide together more smoothly — such as blues from a flower and greens from the leaves. But if you use contrasting hues, like a soft pink from a flower and green from your leaves, you will have to use extremely soft and grayed shades of each where they meet. Otherwise each will look much brighter when placed beside the other.

In (F), where there is a series of shells, each row may be developed a bit differently (but use your darkest values on the outer row to "hold your rug down"). If you are repeating any of your floral colors, choose the quiet and somewhat grayed shades of the flowers — never the brilliant and rich ones — except possibly as an accent where it might be necessary to give it character. Thus your outer row may shade from VERY DARK to MEDIUM, the second row from MEDIUM DARK to MEDIUM LIGHT and the third inner row from MEDIUM to VERY LIGHT. The effect becomes more interesting, in proportion to the variation of your materials.

The main point to keep in mind in all of these borders is the carrying of the development completely around without any sharp jumps or breaks that interfere with the feeling of continuity.

When flowers form a border, as in #97, Page 148 and #104, Page 130 use your chosen colors in their natural sequence on the Color Wheel so that the color as a whole flows together.

No. 494   Young Man's Fancy

No. 530   Summer Bloom

Sometimes ruggers ask: "Where do you get the names for your rugs?" In the earlier days I had a tendency to name the design for the first woman to use the pattern — thus the "Farnsworth Scroll," "Dickson Zig Zag," etc. Then I realized that a design deserved a name symbolic of the detail, and from then on, a pattern sometimes waits several days after it is finished before it is christened. Everyone in the organization helps me to give it a fitting name.

Thus, this one, with its spring-like pansies, narcissus, daffodils and pussy willows, took the name "Young Man's Fancy" (#494 — 24½ x 41) from the poetic:

"In the Spring a young man's fancy
Lightly turns to thoughts of love."

Notice how the rope border twists by using dark shadows against strong highlights. The rope should repeat some color used in the center detail, thus leaf greens, or a soft shade of one of the pansy colors, which might possibly repeat some dominant color in your room, would be the key.

A series of narrow bands, looping in the corners, may be made more interesting by repeating some of the softer colors from a floral center, as in #530 Summer Bloom (36 x 36). These bands should never be bright, however — lest you draw attention from the dominant center.

Actually, the rug illustrated was made as a fireplace rug to cover the opening during the summer. If you are using it for this purpose give consideration to the facing of the fireplace and the woodwork around it, so that the background of the rug will not be dark enough to appear to be an opening to the fireplace.

When made in the proper colors, it could take on a needlepoint effect.

No. 423   Maze Border

A border must always have some relationship to the center, regardless of the design.

Thus, in #423 Maze Border (38 x 82½), the maze border provides detail into which you can bring all the hues used in the leaves, grapes and acorns.

Sometimes this maze is a single line of color of one of your dominating hues, but in this case, be sure that it fluctuates sharply from light to extremely dark.

In one of this design, which is in the hall at Rose Cottage, purple grapes, mauve oak leaves, blue-green woodbine, soft golden brown acorns and red berries lie upon a very light grayish-white background. All of these hues are bound together in the maze. The deepest shades are used first, changing from the plum of the grapes, every five or six inches, into the red of the berries, then back into purple, and thence into the deep blue-greens of the woodbine. Then the lighter shades of the other detail flank both sides of these lines — each one changing every five or six inches so that the maze flows on and on in ever changing hues in the border. Accents of bright light green around the inner edge of the maze border, and deep purple and plum at the edge of the rug add another repetition of color.

Another development which intrigued me in the 1949 Exhibit was rich fall coloring upon a dark inner background. The maze border was played upon a lighter background, but — and this is important — the dark background was again brought out to form an inch wide border at the edge of the rug.

Therefore, whenever using dark inner backgrounds, contrasted with lighter shades in outer areas — bring the dark shades again to the edge of the rug to "hold it down."

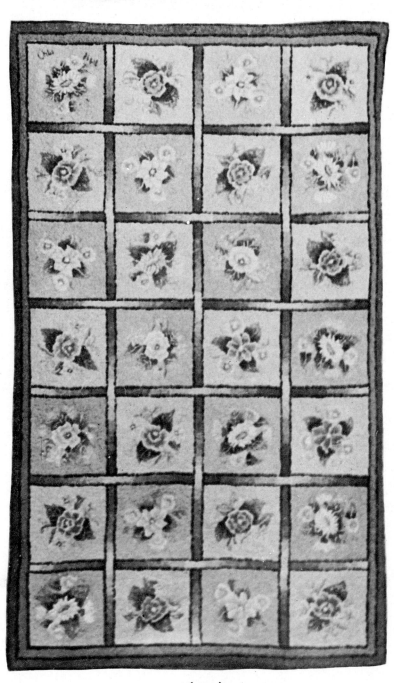

No. PP2   Miniature Bouquet

A border may continue on into the center, as it does in #PP2 Miniature Bouquet (40 x 66), forming intermediate borders around floral centers.

It becomes even more interesting when you highlight and shadow the inner bands, to give a weaving effect, as in this illustration.

In this pattern, there are four different miniature floral pictures. They are not repeated to form diagonal repetition, but rather to give an all-over effect — or, by their position, a little element of surprise.

You may carry out the same element of surprise in your repetition of colors. Thus, the rose need not always be in the same hue wherever it appears. Each little picture may be developed in an individual manner, just so long as you repeat the same general hues throughout the rug, although the proportion of the hue may be varied in each picture.

It is this element of surprise that turns a design from the "set effect" of commercial rugs. Besides, it is more fun to follow your *feeling* about color as you work upon each picture. But watch out for the fundamental rules of good balance — and a certain feeling of repetition.

You will note, too, a very slight difference in the backgrounds of the blocks which give a "suggestive" checkerboard effect, but don't let it be too marked a difference.

A safe hue to use for the bands is your leaf tones — or darker values of your light tinted background.

No. 415　　Birds of Paradise

No. 516　　The Glad Hand

There are many gracious symbols for welcoming your guests — latch strings — brass knockers — but best of all, a Welcome rug inside — spread before the door.

#415 Birds of Paradise (30 x 55½), which smacks of other days, was copied from an old miniature stencil used to decorate the birth and marriage records of an old family Bible. The lettering on the ribbon was my own idea.

Where there is such a variety of detail, repeat your colors again and again. For instance, the bowl might be the hue of the ribbon, and as a glint in the wings of the birds. The roses might tie up to the heart and lettering. The foliage might be in the throat of the birds, or possibly, in a weak tint, the tone of the background. All of the hues might be brought together in the slender gay tail feathers of the birds.

It is full of interesting detail to hook. Even the little red heart which is suspended over the bowl gives one the feeling of a heart warming welcome.

In #516 The Glad Hand (28 x 42½) a little formality is given through the Old English lettering of Welcome, which may be developed in several shades of the soft gray-greens of the poppy leaves. The poppies may be coral, red, mahogany, red-purple or white.

This design may be made even more personal, for you can order the words "to the Maxwells" (or whatever your name may be), to be added to the plain center.

No. 90   PICTORIAL STAIR RUNNERS

--◅{ 198 }▻--

A stair runner may seem like a long task, but not to a true rugger! In fact, because of its repetition it is a good project to turn to, while hooking other rugs under instruction.

If you have the right type of house — like a Cape Cod or similar type of architecture, personalize your runner with #90 Pictorial Stair Runner (23″ wide as shown by the illustration with the widest border — although it may be adjusted to certain other widths).

There is a picture on each rise and the treads may be either plain — hit and miss — or mottled. If using hit and miss background blend your colors closely in similar values, like the second illustration.

There are more than fifty designs to choose from and they can be placed in any order to suit the individual taste.

In one of the runners illustrated you will notice the mottled effect in the background. Several analogous colors were spot-dyed on the material, and then as it was cut straight through its varied tones and hooked at random, the colors blended to give an all-over effect.

In developing the pictures, plan carefully to repeat the same general dominating hue of one picture in various ways in another. Thus, you will notice the little white lamb repeats the clouds and snow of the next picture. The hues of the cornucopia and strawberries are repeated in the feathers of the turkey and the grass and flowers surrounding the frog.

Oh, it's fun to make this type of runner, for there is interest all the way through!

No. 380   ROMANY ROSE (*stair runner*)

A flower bordered stair runner — #380 Romany Rose (22″ wide or adjustable to certain other widths) hangs to the extreme left in this illustration.

In a continuous design like this, one must rely upon variations in the development of the wild roses for interest — for if every one was made exactly alike, it would not only become a most monotonous task, but an uninteresting runner when finished. Thus, one wild rose may be quite dark, another medium, and another extremely light, with possibly one or two other developments making them slightly different from the others but all of one hue. The leaves, too, should vary to off-set the repetition of the pattern.

The area under the flowers may be a definite contrast of value to the hue of your roses, as in this illustration, or the center background may be hooked to the edge of the runner.

When made for a straight flight of stairs it may be advisable to consider making it a little longer than necessary, so that it could run under a rug at the top of the stairs, or be turned back under the first rise. You may then switch the runner each year so that the rise becomes a tread — and thus spread your wear more evenly.

On the floor, the braided rug has a hooked center of #457 Talisman (19 x 22½). #256 Kents Twig (under the table) and #410 Sarah's Bequest (next to it) are illustrated elsewhere in this book.

#341 Dahlia (31¾ x 53) hangs to the extreme right.

The large rug on the wall is not hooked, but is a 319 year old Rya rug made in Upsala, Sweden, loaned for the Exhibit.

No. 514   CASCABEL (*stair runner*)

Impress your guests with your individuality as they enter your home, for through the colors you use in one of these hooked stair runners, your hall may be like no other in the world!

One which will fit into almost any setting — and be most restful to the eye — is #514 Cascabel (27″ wide or adjustable to certain other widths) falling from the window sill in this illustration.

The scrolls are made from neutral grays. The dark grays are used along the center of the scroll flanking the veins, and gradually blend into lighter grays which are almost white at the edge. The veins are terra cotta reds.

The knobs are delicate grayed tints of color — some swinging into delicate green, others in pale blue, lightest lavender, or shell pink.

The background was deep green spot-dyed with some of the colors used in the knobs, and is hooked in such a manner as to give it a mosaic effect.

I would never use a hit and miss background with this type of design — the detail requires simplicity to bring out the beauty of the scrolls.

The large rug nearest to it is #129 Scalloped Scroll (38 x 66). The rug before the dressing table is #336 Fletcher Frost (34 x 56½). The under-arm purse on the dressing table is Bag #16 (6 x 11).

No. 461   VICTORIAN ERA

No. 174   MORNING GLORY BUNNY

Pictorial rugs have their place. They were used on the floors years ago — and in certain settings they seem to be fitting.

#461 Victorian Era (20¼ x 39½) is a type which could also be used for a wall hanging, a reminder of days gone forever!

You can make it quite gay, by dressing the coachman in a red coat and repeating the red in the wheels. The black of his hat and trousers, the thrown-back hood of the carriage, and the harness on the horse, could be a striking contrast to the green trees and grass, or the blue of the sky.

Men would enjoy hooking this pattern!

One of the most popular pictorials is #174 Morning Glory Bunny (30 x 40¼). Mothers love to make it for the children's room. Grandmothers get a great kick out of hooking it for a grandchild. Since all kiddies love bunnies, it would be equally loved by girl or boy.

The chubby bunny in this rug is blended from black and dark gray shadows into very light gray highlights. It is crouched in the grass of varied greens, so peaceful against the fleecy clouded pale blue sky beyond. Soft mulberry pink morning glories which twine across diagonal corners are contrasted with bronzy green leaves and tiny rose and yellow blossoms. A medium gray background forms the wide frame to the picture.

YOUR children will pass it on to THEIR children!

Flowers from the woods form a repeat diamond design in #392 Wild Flowers (32 x 56) and make this pattern an unusually good choice for a young girl's or boy's room. Nice for grown-ups too!

Keep the background beneath each flower plain, and either quite light or very dark, which will dramatize the flower detail.

In the intervening diamonds you will note the suggestive outline of a fern frond which forms delicate detail between the flowers. In the pattern, the fern fronds are sketched in lightly with skips in the lines, and this is the way it was intended to be hooked. If you develop these fern fronds in too strong tones, or fill them in solid, the eye may be attracted to this detail rather than the real picture of the design.

Soft greens — a repetition of those you use in the various leaves — are good for the fern detail in these intervening diamonds.

The line which marks off the diamonds should be a dark value and of the same hue you intend to use for the outer border. A soft dark dull green is always good, because of its tie-up to the leaf shades.

There is a good opportunity to repeat your hues in the various pictures to bind them together. For instance, the light lavender in the thistle may be used again, and also deepened, in the wild iris and the purple asters. The pink of the lady's-slipper may form pinkish accents in the water lily, and may be deepened for the wild rose. The false foxglove (under thistle) may be a softer yellow than the deep gold of the ox-eyed daisies. The blue of the harebells may be repeated in the purple fringed gentian. The reds and greens of the jack-in-the-pulpit may be reflected in the pitcher plant.

The material you choose may give a feeling of antiquity to your rug. Memory lingers on this rug, shown at one of my Exhibits, which was hooked in mellowed materials that gave it an almost aged appearance.

It is #425 Richmont Scroll (54 x 88). Its outer background was old black material which had a very dull tone. The scrolls were made from rose-red paisley shawls with dull-green veins and accents.

The middle background between the two sets of scrolls was a very fady light grayish-blue, and the inner background around the floral center was a soft bluish-gray. Then the black outer background was repeated under the floral detail, as was often seen in many of the oldest rugs.

All of the floral detail was keyed to the paisley reds.

Notice how part of the floral detail was permitted to extend over on the lighter area. The dark was dropped where flower and leaf touched to form a breaking point.

It is always so surprising to see how color changes a design. I have only recently seen a beautiful development of this pattern in a strikingly different effect. Rose, mauve and purple were used for most of the flowers and scrolls, against leaves of varied grays with highlights of almost white. The inner background was a grayish-white — with a light gray intermediate area and a medium gray outer background.

There are certain designs which make charming companions for your antiques — and #304 Miller Floral (50 x 67½) is one of them. In this illustration it takes on a feeling of mid-victorian.

Notice the mottled effect in the background. This is a combination of two slightly different navy blues — mottled and blended together in an all-over effect which results in a subtly interesting background.

The rich reds of the roses in the center and corners were the dominating bright hue in this rug. Notice how they soften and lighten at the petals' edges. All other flowers were subdued to this red.

The large clusters of phlox or hydrangea which appear in this design often pick up and repeat all the varied hues of the other flowers. Thus, each little blossom differs somewhat from its neighbors, one swinging to the pinky-lavenders reflecting the purple of a tulip — another blending into lavender-blues, repeating the blue of a padula — and others of reddish-pink, suggestive of the darker shades of a rose. A flat appearance in this group of tiny blossoms may be avoided if the lighter values are used at the center of the group or at one side, throwing the rest of the blossoms into shadows through darker values.

The floral bouquet is full of strange padulas and small sprigs of leaves and curling tendrils at its extremities which are fascinating to hook.

This design is also available with a border that joins the floral corners (#304A, same size) and thus permits a two-toned background.

GEOMETRICS

Don't think geometrics will be too simple to hook. If you do, what a surprise you will have coming to you! Because, if you are going to make them beautiful — and they can be truly lovely — they require considerable planning. Not until you begin to fill the lines with color do you see the full possibilities of even the simplest design.

Don't get the mistaken idea that the repetition of a geometric makes it uninteresting. Your whole life is made up of repetition, but you keep life interesting by breaking into that repetition at irregular and unexpected intervals. It's the constant change of routine and trips away from home that make you glad to get back to your old rut. It's too many nights out that make you really appreciate your comfortable bed and a long night's rest. In short, it's the contrast of two extremes that arouses appreciation of both. That is one of the secrets of the charm in geometrics — when they are well planned in color they provide contrast in texture, tone and color. So whether you keep to the simplicity of light and dark shades of one color, or work out an interesting contrast in more than one color, you should break up the repetition by changes in texture and tone.

Thus, instead of using one dark value of a color over and over again in the same identical position, use one that varies slightly from it — a little lighter for the same detail in another motif. Therefore don't ever worry if you run short of material in this type of design. Laugh and be glad! Let your ingenuity in improvising, where you have a shortage of material, prevent your rug from becoming boring.

There is something, too, about these simple designs that makes them particularly fitting for certain interiors, especially with traditional or antique furniture. Geometrics can repeat soft tones from walls or gay colors from draperies. They are exceptionally appropriate for boys' rooms.

But they *do* require thought — advanced thought. Once you get the rug well planned, you can relax and thoroughly enjoy your hooking because it will present no more problems. That is one reason why it is a very good idea to keep a geometric in your frame at all times, to turn to. When you run into a problem on your floral or scroll design and need time and thought to solve it, you can turn to your geometric and really make time on it while you are awaiting the solution.

In geometrics particularly, color should not be used in a way to tire the eye or confuse the mind. Most geometrics call for a certain area in which your somewhat neutral materials may be used as a place for the eye to rest. Thus your light tans shaded down into your medium browns are excellent for this purpose. Or your varied grays, even if they have a diagonal weave or a little pattern in the material, are excellent foils for color. Save them both.

The second group of materials to store away for geometrics is a plain variety of colors. No matter how small the quantity, if it is in the general hue that you intend to use, tuck it away, for it can be used in small areas and thus spread over the whole rug.

The third group of materials to save is well balanced plaids, mixtures, patterned or figured materials. Anything which has a pattern, so that when it is cut and hooked in as a filler, gives an interesting effect in a small area and adds character to the design.

When you have completed your flowered rugs, pack away the left-overs among those of similar colors to be used in a geometric later. You will find that all these little scraps will fit into your rugs beautifully, no matter what pattern you choose.

Don't close your mind to geometrics. Even if they have not appealed to you before, they may hold a delightful surprise for you in the future.

The technique for a geometric is a little different from the flower and scroll patterns. You must be particular to hook with all straight lines, and to make square corners in turning on any right angle. If a design has a block or square cornered motif, hook the outlines of that first, to form a "fence" so you will keep the contour of it when working in and around it. Then maintain these straight lines by balancing your hooking — that is, by first hooking on one side with the color which is to be used within the line, and then on the other side, until you have two or three lines on either side. Then the rest of your hooking will not pack and shove these lines out of shape.

In developing a design that is made up of blocks, use a variety of textures and shades even though you are confining them to practically one hue, hooking one line of one kind of material against one of another. This slight variation between texture or shade helps break up the solidity of your color, and gives a much more interesting effect.

In a design where there are intervening motifs, or details within a motif, they should be planned in such colors and values as to support and bring to completion the design as a whole. In other words, the smaller details should not "jump out" or appear spotty over the rug.

Geometrics should really be soothing and of delightful variation, with the intricacy or simplicity of the design only apparent upon closer inspection. Never should you find yourself tracing its lines, in here — out there — around this — under that — so that the thing remains with you long after, to torment your mind as to where it finally ended. This is what may happen if you permit either material or color to take on too much importance, or be left unbalanced.

Of course the most important point in geometrics is the choice of color. You can use a variety of values or shades of one color, relying upon contrast of light against dark for interest. Or you can blend any two or three analogous hues together, such as yellow-green into green and then into blue-green, in their varied values and shades, and they will flow together. Or you can use complementary contrasts, (that is, two extreme opposites on your Color Wheel), but since each will appear more striking when used with the other, subdue one, and stress the other.

The art of arriving at the desired effect through the use of color is possibly achieved only through actual experience. Therefore never count as loss the failure of getting into your rugs the exact color desired. Of course you must turn these failures to success by observation of what one color will do when hooked against another. If, for instance, you have put into your rug a color which deadens and takes away the vitality of the surrounding shades, make a mental note of it, for it is by trial and error one learns more quickly. Soon you will find you have stored up a fund of practical knowledge on color which you would not have thought possible.

Slight contrasts in geometrics do not have much appeal. It is the artistic combination of a small amount of intense colors and their shadows and gay highlights that makes the difference between a distinguished and a commonplace rug. Thus, pastels do not work out well in geometrics — they have an insipid tone. But mingle them with neighboring hues of greater intensity and they will take on more character.

The general background tone, or in other words, the color which will probably be used in the greatest area, should be decided upon first, so choose somewhat neutral shades and use them as a foil for your other hues. Now look about you for the dominating colors in your room. Choose two or three to be emphasized and supplement with all their varied values and shades. Remember that the intensity of color should increase and the contrast of values should grow sharper at most important points of your design.

Don't be confused by my previous comment that dyeing a material with its complementary color will dull it — and my statement now that hooking a color against its complement (opposite) will sharpen both colors. It is still true that a tint of blue-green dye will dull turkey red material, but contrariwise, blue-green material hooked next to a bright red will make both appear even more luminous.

In planning any block design, sort your materials so that all those that have any signs of your dominating color, whether they be plaids, mixtures, checks or plain, will be in one pile, while those that have any suggestion of the color of your second hue should be in a second pile.

Now in a block, such as (A) in the following illustration, hook each line of a different material, all of which might lean toward green, for instance. Thus the sequence might be a light check or plaid — a medium tweed — a dark plain material — a light tweed — a dark check or plaid, etc. This will give you a thready effect. Then in the part of the block marked (B), you could similarly combine the varied materials of your second hue.

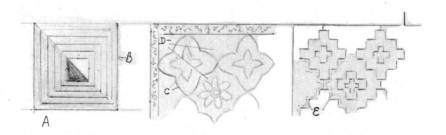

Or you could make (A) of the darker values of your two hues, and (B) of the combined lighter values, with accents of the two hues in the triangular centers.

In this type of design, there are those having intervening motifs. They provide an opportunity for complementary contrast, but since they are striking together, they really require simple and plain backgrounds.

In (C) the two outlines of the corner motif should reflect

something from the conventional rose that forms the intervening figure. Likewise there should be something brought into the conventional rose from the body of the first motif.

In hooking the background around the conventional motif and between the larger motifs, as in (D), it is much better to hook at random, after running your background color around the edge of the border.

But if all the detail of the design follows angular lines, as in (E), it is better to follow these lines in hooking background.

Since I have already covered this subject at more length in another publication "The Gist of Geometrics,"* I have written here only the main essentials of such a design.

---

*A complete listing of all publications by Pearl K. McGown is to be found in the back of the book.

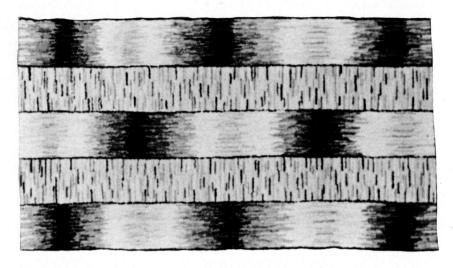

No. 122   Sunshine and Shadow

No. 412   Wheeler Centenary

So many times ruggers will write me: "I want a design to use up odds and ends."

A little forethought will produce some interesting effects in #122 Sunshine and Shadow (25¼ x 45).

Can you visualize all your dark greens and blue-greens blending gradually into lighter greens and yellow-greens and thence back into the dark greens and blue-greens again, in the side and center band of this pattern?

Can you see all your varied light background shades interspersed with pleasing contrasting colors, including the greens of the other bands, in the cross-wise bands?

The same principle may be applied to other hues.

Bright colors if used in small areas give jewel tones that glint and glow in a design like #412 Wheeler Centenary (24½ x 39½).

Keep the background plain and simple — and a decided contrast to your detail. In the line which marks off your squares avoid brilliance, because it is not this straight line to which you wish to call attention.

Use your brilliant colors as an outline to the small detail — or as a filler to the smallest objects in the squares.

Develop the two designs somewhat differently — but repeat enough of the color of one in the other to accent and bind the two together. Thus the flower in one might be the largest scroll in the other.

It is variety, not only in values but in grayed and intense hues, that lends interest to geometrics, and #86 Vermont Geometric (40 x 70) is a good illustration to show the dark and light effects which you may hook into the details.

In the rug illustrated a complementary contrast of soft greens and terra cotta reds was used — the greens dominating in the dark outer background — and — in a very grayed medium shade — in the background beneath the rosette. Light neutral shades provide a pleasing contrast in the background of the cross.

Terra cotta accents the outline of the cross and provides contrasts in the green diamond within. Likewise, the terra cotta rosettes include repetitions of the greens.

Notice the extremely light values, possibly neutrals, used near the center of the rosettes, and to form another accenting line to the contour of the cross and the outline of the intervening motif.

Any two complementary colors are good in a geometric, providing you have several values of both, and let one of the hues dominate somewhat over the other, through unequal quantity.

Analogous hues will also develop geometrics in some unusual effects. As a rule, the fewer colors used — with variations in the values — the more beautiful the rug.

Slight differences in the background tones in this design, and in many other geometrics, are quite permissible so long as they do not appear spotty.

Plaids and mixtured materials are excellent for small detail like the centers of these two motifs.

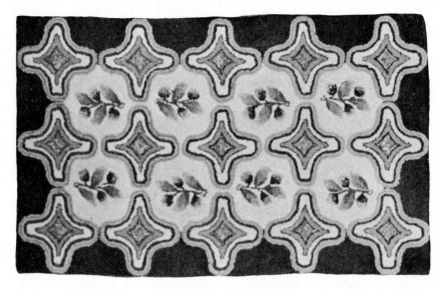

No. 256   KENT'S TWIG

No. 344   WHIPPLE

It is a conventional design like #256 Kents Twig (27 x 45) that offers wonderful possibilities for using up the accumulation of odd amounts of material from hooking other rugs. Now I do not mean that you put your colors in without any regard for planning. But suppose you have a variation of good reds to reddish-pinks — a good variation of greens, and all sorts of beige, tans, browns of varied values. Perhaps not too much of this — but quite a lot of that!

The varied reds may be used for this little conventional blossom — shading each according to your quantity — but spreading them — with some thought toward balance. Your greens may vary in the leaf detail. Your browns from dark to light may develop the conventional figure between, but use flashes of your reds and greens in some small detail within them. It is not absolutely necessary that the same identical tan be used in the same identical position in each figure. The variance in them adds interest to the final effect.

This is also true of #344 Whipple (29 x 48½). Vary the conventional flowers. Though they may be of the same hues, the proportion of values of the hue may change — as long as you avoid any spotty effects.

Something of their hue should be repeated somewhere within the intervening motif to pull the two together. Likewise use something from this motif to accent the center of the conventional flower either as filler or outline.

You can almost see this variance in the illustration of this design.

Be sure that the outside border is related to the motifs within.

No. 161C   WATSON SQUARE

There is a certain type of furnishing like an antique setting, that calls for either the geometric, quaint, or primitive design.

A geometric, like #161C Watson Square (31 x 44½) fits well into such a scheme. Its interesting straight borders broken up by diamonds and square intersections offer a resting place for all those delightful plaids you have been saving.

The rug illustrated was made for an antique pine bedroom. The variance in the fingered motifs and their irregular backgrounds was planned to give the rug a century old appearance. Its balance of light and dark values is also a good point to notice in this rug.

It is best to use slightly different values of one hue or not more than two (and those two should be neighbors on your color wheel) for the dominating "fingered" motif, for otherwise the rug might become spotty.

The center of this motif, its outline, and the outline and fillers of the diamonds and intersecting squares all offer opportunities for repeating your colors throughout the rug, to form unity.

This same design, but turned to form large diamonds in an all-over pattern, is available as #161 Watson Diamond.

The rug at the extreme left is #251 Antique Leaf.

Notice the hooked table top under the lamp. It is CS #201 and has a plain center for just this purpose.

No. 251   ANTIQUE LEAF

A geometric, or conventional design may bring out a double or intervening pattern, such as #251 Antique Leaf (36 x 72).

It is made up of twelve inch squares, but when you hook the corners you form an intervening diamond also.

Unless you use a real dark hue to outline and maintain the square influence, as in this illustration, your design will turn to diamonds.

In this illustration, you will note, too, that additional interest has been given to the pattern by using light hit and miss corners on the light background squares, and dark hit and miss corners on the dark background squares. This lends a certain transparency effect to the design as a whole. This is one reason why geometrics become so fascinating — because, in the application of your colors and the choice of your values, you bring out effects not always intentional.

In this pattern you use your intensity of color in the leaves, flashing repetitions of their hues in the hit and miss corners which are usually developed of all sorts of somewhat neutral mixtures, plaids, tweeds and plain materials, changing each line of hooking to a different shade or texture, but using all of them in shades which will give a brownish or greenish cast (or any other desired hue) to this part of your pattern.

I like the way some of these leaves are shaded, using darker values along one side of the vein shading out to a light edge, and lighter values along the other side of the vein shading to a dark edge. Repeat the general hue of one leaf as the veining of another — or, in its tints, as a tip to another.

No. P16   Sampler

No. P14   Xmas Tree

Bag No. 13

Bag No. 5

Bag No. 13

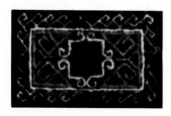

Bag No. 18

Bag No. 7

Hooking may be given the effect of "needlepoint" if you will cut your material fine and hook close and low. Thus, this finer technique is often applied to detail which calls for minute accent of shadow and highlight — or in pieces which are normally near the eye, such as bags.

The pride of a rugger is often displayed in her careful development of flower detail as in this SAMPLER, which she often frames to suit the decorative plan of a room. Its several kinds of flowers are a challenge to her artistry in the use of color.

Scenic pictures offer an opportunity to "paint with rags." With a gay muffler around his throat and an axe in his hand, this woodsman drags home the Xmas tree to brighten the little cabin, from which soft yellow lighted windows indicate a warm spirit within. It's fun to "paint" blue and purple shadows into the snow, cover the river with ice, and drop snow flakes upon the branches of the evergreens in the distance. Warmth is usually given to the picture through the sunset sky beyond the trees.

Smart women will make bags of their coat or suit materials — with a shorter strap for the matron, or shoulder straps for young girls, as in #13.

The underarm bags are most attractive! The color of the dahlia on #5 may be like the dress with which it is worn. Or if made of white, with delicate tints of color, it will be suitable for several dresses. Gay Oriental colors in the design of bag #18 are played against a black background. I have one of this design made with a white background, during a summer when I had three dresses of quite definitely different colors. We used all three hues so that it could be worn with any of them. The background of bag #7 may match a tailored suit or coat, with any desired color accent repeated in the rose.

CS 213 Phlox

CS 171 Dahlias

FS 33

FS 32

Pillows may be soft and pliable if you are careful to cut your material fine and hook low.

The lighter one is #CS213. Its phlox of white, delicate pink and dainty lavender are lovely against a soft light green background. The background material has also been used for a plain unhooked back and to make the shirred wide bands which join front to back.

In the darker pillow (#CS171) the dahlias are rich wine and greenish-gold, set off with yellow-green foliage against a grayish-beige background. A rich wine velvet was used for the back and the plain side bands which joined the two together. The edge is corded with the velvet.

Most any chair seat design may be turned into a pillow, although there are several designs made for just this purpose.

I have a weakness for footstools and these are two of my favorites. You can find these old footstools in antique shops and they finish up beautifully.

The square one is of mahogany (#FS33). Its roses are a soft coral pink with other floral detail in yellows, peach and yellow-greens — a nice contrast to the medium old blue background.

Every kiddie loves to sit on this three legged stool (#FS32) which is in my Studio. It has a black background with a rich red rose and yellow-green leaves.

In covering a footstool the design should be in good proportion to the top of the stool — and allowance made for the extra background necessary to cover the sides.

No. 552 & 552A   THE PRINCESS (*chair upholstery*)

Hooking may be applied to a chair as upholstery, but you must cut quite fine and hook low if it is to be pliable enough to be moulded to the chair.

You will notice in this finger carved walnut chair to which #552 The Princess (25 x 26 seat) and #552A (14 x 14½ back) have been applied, that it follows the rhythmic curve in that part which fits into the base of the seat.

The pattern is made so that you hook around the area which must fit into the side back pieces of the chair back.

The colorings in the shell-pink rose, muted purple tulips and greenish-blue forget-me-nots give it a needlepoint effect. The pansies repeat the purple and pinks of the rose and tulip and the leaves are the usual needlepoint blue-greens and yellow-greens.

The illustration also gives you an idea of the slight fluctuation in the background which is a deep "raisin" shade — a reddish brown or brownish-wine. This chair upholstery has been covered by a back issue of the Letter Service.

There are a few other similar designs, but of course much depends upon the size of your chair. The design should always be in good proportion to the size of the seat and back.

If your chair does not have an upholstered back, you will find that there are many of my chair seat patterns which will make similar upholsteries for a seat and may be ordered on larger burlaps for such a purpose.

ORIENTALS

Some people are surprised that we hook Oriental rugs. Others express the feeling that if they are going to have Orientals, they prefer the real ones.

Now it is said that in the olden days, when the sea captains came home from abroad with their treasures, they brought beautiful Oriental rugs to their wives. Other women, whose husbands were fishermen or men who had not the opportunity to travel, copied the Oriental designs of their friends and then hooked them for themselves.

In any event, Edward Sands Frost, the first commercial designer of hooked rugs, had a great many Orientals among his patterns, so we do know that they were in demand from eighty to a hundred years ago.

Men love to hook Orientals, probably because after they have set the colors in the various borders, and in a section of the center and end medallions, the rest is a matter of repeat. Also, it may be because they can use brighter colors in Orientals, for the play of one color against another is most intriguing.

Among my designs there are two types — The Turkish Oriental, made up of angular motifs and the Persian Oriental, made up of curving lines with fanciful floral and leaf detail.

My "Objectives in Orientals,"* illustrates nine patterns of the former type, and explains in great detail, the meaning of the motifs, and how each is developed. Therefore, I shall only refer to the main facts to consider in the average design of this type.

Before you start any Oriental, sort your materials, so you can determine your general dark, medium and light shades of the chosen hues. Choose those which are going to provide an interesting Oriental harmony which will tie in with your other Orientals.

Plaids, checks, tweeds and mixtures are excellent as fillers in the smaller detail. They give variety without too many colors.

Use brilliant colors, if any, for the smaller detail.

The colors which are usually copied from the old rugs are red, crimson, scarlet, rose, saffron yellow, old gold, rich yellow, brownish-copper, terra cotta, cinnamon, ruddy brown-gray, pale grayish-green, navy, royal, old blues and purples. Sometimes but one hue is used for the entire rug but always in contrasting light against dark effect. Often when two colors are used one dominates the other to give a more or less monotone effect.

Most people today who are hooking Orientals want them to reflect and repeat the general coloring of surrounding Orientals. Thus the dominating hue of a nearby Oriental might be repeated for the plain field of the center; the secondary color for the most prominent details, and the supporting or less important colors for outline and accents. Each hue, however, should be repeated again and again as outline, filler for detail, for background and border lines.

Borders are of great importance in Orientals. They may be very broad, but sometimes so narrow as to appear to be only a line or two. Yet each must have true individuality.

Let the law of contrast be your guide. Use duplicate and triplicate outlines for the figures, thus breaking up their solidity. Let the outline of one motif be the filler of another. In these outlines play contrast against contrast of both value and hue.

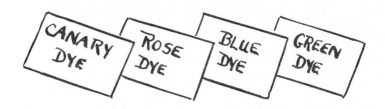

---

*A complete listing of all publications by Pearl K. McGown is to be found in the back of the book.

No. 134   Frost Oriental

When I published my pamphlet "Objectives in Orientals," I described my rug of this design — #134 Frost Oriental (37 x 72) — which is on exhibit at Rose Cottage. I illustrated each little motif in every border, relating in detail the way the colors were used to develop the entire rug.

One is never too sure that another can visualize the color of which one may speak — even if great care is used in defining it. I have, therefore, always been amazed when others have followed my description to the point of producing a rug almost identical with mine.

In the rug illustrated you can easily imagine how plaids and mixtures could be used as fillers in the little motifs in the two outside borders, and repeated again in many of those appearing in the center detail.

Notice too, how the plain dark borders around the outside are used again as background areas in the end panels, the keys at the ends of the center, and in the center motif.

It is easy to imagine that the little Maltese crosses in the inner border could be repeated again in the "combs" which surround the medallion center.

It is thus that one needs only about 12 values of two or three different hues for an entire Oriental design. But it is in using these varied hues and values in different ways — sometimes as a filler — other times as one of two or more outlines to a motif — or sometimes as background of a border or small area, that provides a repetition which gives unity to the design as a whole.

The colors of an oriental hooked rug are usually influenced by either real orientals, or by the dominating hues of a room.

In #411 Maltese Oriental (29½ x 50) the background is well covered by detail. There is very little plain area except in the background around the center motif. Therefore, repeat your backgrounds over and over, and choose but a few hues, and use them over and over again, in varied values and intensities of color, in different ways to develop the motifs.

In the one illustrated, you will notice that the dark background which has been used at each end of the center and in the wide border, has again been used as a narrow border between the two light borders, and finally at the edge. In the same manner, the light center background has been used again and again for the three narrow borders. Thus, this repetition of backgrounds (they may be two slightly different values of the same hue, or two very slightly different shades of a light beige or cream) brings unity to the rug as a whole and offsets the busyness of the pattern.

In the same manner the colors chosen for the rug may be used as a filler for the motifs in one border and as an outline to a motif in another. In this way contrasting colors will be massed in one place and appear in delicate tracery in another. Thus, in the wide border the color of the vine which meanders through the border may be repeated as outlines or small fillers in other details within the same border.

Likewise, the filler and outlines of the center motif may be reversed in the little diamonds at the ends.

No. 545   JULIE

#545 Julie (24 x 36) was inspired by a real Oriental in the Pink Palace
Museum in Memphis, Tenn., during an exhibit there.

Notice how the light value in one of the outer borders is repeated as the
center background. The feeling of the light to dark values that form the
barber stripe border has been put into the dark and light reciprocal border.

The dark values of the background in the latter border and at the edge
of the rug are brought into small areas in the corner motifs, but in the center,
where the contrast would have been too striking against the light area surrounding it, these dark values have been lightened to avoid a hard outline to
the center motif.

The balance of light and dark values is important in all designs.

MODERN

It is not easy for me to go modern in design, and I cannot get enthusiastic over the abstract. Is it to be expected that we must swing with all new trends?

I feel like Thoreau that:

*"If I do not keep step with others it is because I hear a
different drummer. Let a man step to the music which
he hears, however measured and however far away."*

Therefore, I can design only that which is within me.

Yet, many grandmothers have said to me, "I want to make a rug for my granddaughter. Her home is very modern. She is not interested in scrolls and flowers." So, I have tried to meet this trend part way (perhaps not too successfully) with what might serve as a spot-light of interest on a very plain floor in a modern room, and keep grandmother's hands busy!

Such a point of interest is often before a fireplace, or possibly before a davenport which might be the center conversational area.

Illustrated herein are two of them, #520 Southern Belle and #540 Dogwood, but there are a few others, like #534 Sea Grapes which was illustrated in McCall's Magazine (Jan. '51) in an article about my work. This design was inspired by its tree-like shrub in southern Florida and might well be used in a modern setting.

I have found, however, that the treatment of color in a modern design must of necessity be quite different from our usual methods. A flat development of the design, in almost monochromatic colorings, with very subtle borders, has seemed to work out best.

At one of my Annual Exhibits, a very modern Interior Decorator arranged some furniture groupings and chose geometrics of bold design and simple coloring, expressing the feeling that they would fit in well with modern settings.

Because of its bold pattern, #520 Southern Belle (34 x 60) should have a dominant place of interest in a room, and have little or no competition with other rugs. It was made to be used before a fireplace in a wall to wall carpeted room. For that reason the color of the background should be a lighter or darker value, or a duller, or only slightly brighter shade of the carpet.

Forget realism in choosing your colors, and develop this design in an exaggerated effect, if necessary, to bind it to your room.

In the rug illustrated, notice that the mahogany pink turn-overs of the petals and the new small leaves of the magnolia are a complementary contrast to the greenish-blues in some of the leaves. A subtle reflection of the delicate greenish-blue is brought over into some of the magnolia's petals. It is this imaginative treatment that delights the eye. The extreme highlights in some of the leaves are another exaggeration which adds to the modern feeling.

In the pattern, the detail extends in a few places into a 2 inch plain border, but it has been eliminated in this development. When it is used as designed, it should be subtly darker than the background, and, if on a wall to wall carpet, of a shade which will blend with the hue of the carpet.

But this design is also used with a hard wood or other type of uncovered floor, where the surrounding area does not present an additional color problem.

#540 Dogwood (34 x 65) will fit into a modern setting, where line of design or development of color must be kept simple.

Since the dogwood may be somewhat neutral (if white), you may repeat a soft subdued shade of a dominant color in a room, for background, if desired.

But because the flowers are neutral, give them some interest by suggestive colors in the little curving indentations of the petals. Delicate greenish-yellows, pinks, lavenders, blues, or even grays, will give them this interest, and still keep the effect of a white blossom. The centers may be more colorful and are often made in chartreuse (usually dyed over a black and white check or mixture). The blossoms which are in profile may be shadowed by using more of light gray and less of white for their petals.

If a definite color is not used in the background, the leaves may be any pleasing colorful contrast to the natural flowers — for instance, quite bright blue-greens or yellow-greens, depending upon your color scheme.

Note how the detail extends just a little into the border at the edge. The border should be a subtle change to the inner background — not a hard and sharp contrast of value, nor a contrasting color to it, but they should really melt together.

Pink dogwood with blue-green leaves against a creamy background would also make a pleasing modern interpretation of this pattern, but avoid the use of too many light values. Give it weight and strength through dark values in leaves and branches.

No. 527   Omar Khayyam

The Persian influence of curving lines and conventionalized flowers and leaves is shown in #527 Omar Khayyam (60 x 84).

Don't let yourself think of a design like this as too intricate to hook. Actually, it does not present the color problems of many other types of pattern. After you have planned a few units in each border and one-fourth of the center, the rest is repetitive.

The main idea is to use the same hues over and over again in different ways in all of the varied detail in the rug.

For instance, you will note the background in the two narrow borders is like the scrolls which cut off the corners and surround the center medallion. The terra cotta reds of the little flowers in the narrow borders are repeated in the conventionalized flower in the wide border and in the various units in the center.

The purples in the wide border are repeated in the scrolls and units around the medallion, and in some of the corner flowers.

The background of the center medallion is repeated in the spandrels.

Notice the reddish edges to the leaves of the wide border. An imaginative detail! This is the type of design which is full of detail that permits the creative use of color in a fanciful manner and satisfies the rugger.

PLANNING YOUR RUG

The background of your hooked rug is the most important feature and should be determined before you start to hook!

The reason for this is that all your colors may be either subdued or heightened by your choice of background. Therefore, you must know what it is to be, before you start. It is always advisable to hook a little bit of background around the detail as you work, so you will know what is going to happen to the contour and edges of the detail. Sometimes you may have to accent them with lighter or darker values to save them from the background.

A background that has a slight fluctuation or change of tone is more interesting than one made from one solid shade of material. The answer to this is that we tire of monotony. However, do be careful not to combine two or more materials in such a way that you are conscious of the background before you are of the detail, for in that case you have made it of far too great importance. You can get this fluctuation by spot-dyeing material — not strikingly — but just enough so there is a little variation as you hook it in. Or you can get it from two materials of great similarity. For instance, in dark backgrounds, you will find that if you have two navy blues which are only slightly different, you will get a much more interesting effect than you would from one navy.

Don't make definite S's, or any other figures or motifs in the backgrounds that will draw your attention as you look at the rug as a whole. But if you are using two or more kinds of material, hook in a slightly mottled manner, working at random, so the two become thoroughly blended. If you are making a subtle pattern in your background, such as a honeycomb, strive for a subdued all-over effect which will not be too apparent to the eye.

Don't use strong colors as background — unless with neutral or extremely grayed hues in the detail. If you want a colorful background with definite color in detail, subdue the background material to an extremely dark value of low intensity — or a medium extremely grayed hue — or a light and delicate tint. avoid high color in *both* detail and background in the same rug.

While black and all extremely dark hues make excellent outside background *areas*, don't use them as a hard frame-like *border* for a rug, UNLESS they have some connection with center detail.

If you are hooking on an all light background in a design that offers no scroll or other detail to change to another background shade at the edge of your rug, then either gradually darken your light background to at least a medium shade at the edge, or bring three or four lines of your soft subdued colors from your floral center to the edge of your rug. This will add a little weight and hold it down.

The center of your design is the center point of interest and all detail radiating from the center point should balance in an opposite or triangular manner. Thus, if there were but two flowers alike in the center, one would balance the other, although you can always exaggerate the highlights on one more than the other without losing balance.

Two flowers alike or similar, at each end of a bouquet, should be balanced, either in the same hue or in the same values of two different hues. Any flower which drops from the center point to the right hand lower side of a bouquet should balance diagonally some flower on the upper left hand side. Likewise, those of the upper right hand side should balance in some way those diagonally opposite in the lower left hand side. If the flowers in these positions are not identical, the colors in them may be — thus a light blue pansy could balance a light blue petunia.

Then there is the triangular balance. In many of my own original designs, I have taken care of this triangular balance through placing the various flowers in a three cornered manner. Watch for these triangles, and make the flowers in these positions of the same hue — those nearest the center of the darker values

No. 458   Sassafras Scroll

DO be subtle about mottling materials together in forming backgrounds. In #458 Sassafras Scroll (36 x 62) it has been done in an irregular manner to break up the inner background. The darker shade shadows the area inside the scroll and in a still darker value under the floral bouquet. It forms a note of interest, yet it is not enough to hold the attention too long from the main detail of the design.

There is a feeling of continuity in the scroll border and a consistent repetition from center to the outer areas of the design through both flowers and leaves.

I remember one of this design that had a dark mahogany brown outer background — a mottled (dyed in fluctuating manner) mahogany-tan inner background, with a scroll of soft mahogany on the outer side, and delicate blue-green on the inner side. It was most artistic, because the two hues were brushed together in such a manner that the mahogany side was highlighted with the delicate blue-green, and the light blue-green side was brushed at the base with deep values of the mahogany. Thus the two hues fused enough so that the scroll was not split. It was delightful!

This is a particularly easy pattern to do, and a good one for the novice. The scrolls may repeat or be in a similar hue to the flower hue of your choice, and be veined with your leaf tones, as in this illustration. The background may be all the same, if preferred.

You may use color in your background, even with a contrasting colorful scroll, if you subdue background to scroll.

For instance, I once saw this principle applied in a most harmonious manner in #300 St. Gaudens (32½ x 61½) when the mauve scroll gradually blended from its deep knobs into a light mauve pink tip, against a very subdued sagey-green outer background.

Because the two hues were of unequal intensity and their values had little contrast it had a most pleasing effect.

The mauve was carried into the centers and corners through the roses, and all the other floral detail was in subdued purples, blues and delicate yellows. The dull sagey-green of the outer background was intensified to provide bronzy and yellow-green foliage — lovely against the light inner background.

In another instance, where a rosy-rust scroll was used against a duller dark rust outer background, the scroll had the tendency of sinking away into the outer background, and left the light detail along the inner side of the scroll to form a delicate feathery frame to the picture within. The study of color helps you to visualize what is going to happen to your detail before you hook your colors together in your rug.

Where did the name of this rug come from? I was travelling in Vermont and found a woman who was repairing an extremely old rug of this design, for St. Gaudens, the sculptor!

No. 420   GARDEN OF EDEN

Color, when properly used, may add interest and beauty to the background of a rug. In #420 Garden of Eden (36 x 75) the background is a deep, but somewhat subdued wine. Notice that most of the flowers and the grapes are in some light shade of the same hue as the background, though they blend down into darker values, thus giving this part of the detail a more or less monochromatic feeling.

Notice too the simplicity of coloring in developing the greater area of the scroll border, shading from green to blue, or vice versa. Notice how it is brought over into the contrasting detail.

One of this design, which I remember very well, had a very light inside background with a shadowed effect beneath the floral center which gave it an additional relationship to the dark outside background.

The torch-like detail will slide into the rest of the scroll easily when it is made of neighboring hues.

The tendrils attached to the grape detail at the two ends may be turned and twisted to form your initials and possibly the year you make the rug.

Some ruggers always "sign" their rugs in some such manner, but DO be subtle about it. If no part of the detail offers a chance to put them in unobtrusively — or if you personally prefer larger letters or dates — use a hue and value only slightly different from that in the area around it, so that it is not too noticeable.

and those at the extremities, or more distant from the center, of lighter values. Of course there are always those who will follow rules too strictly and miss the "exceptions to every case." They will probably repeat in too perfect a way the exact values and hues of a flower. Others, more artistic, will follow the "exceptions," and while repeating the general hue, and the right values, to a great extent will still introduce that "something different" which makes their work outstanding. I have in mind now the case of one woman who makes three purple tulips practically in the same hues and values — while another will make two of them very similar, but perhaps in the third swing her purple tulip through accented shadows a little toward a bluish-purple, or through highlights a little toward the orchidy-pink.

A variety of VALUES in your rug makes it much more interesting! Thus all light values — or all extremely dark values — or even all medium values in any one rug become monotonous. Accent contrast of values in the floral bouquets particularly, by using a wide range of values in the leaf detail — not necessarily all in one leaf. Make some leaves much lighter and some much darker than others.

Avoid the use of one color in one detail that has not been repeated anywhere else in the rug, because it will be spotty and have no relationship to anything else.

Two of the most important words with the greatest meaning, in the development of your rugs, are REPETITION and CONTINUITY. If you use these two in your color plan, you will arrive at a unified rug. Naturally the center or more important flower should be of the dominating hue, but not necessarily of the same values. Repeat something of this same color in some of the less important flowers — or as a vein in a leaf. Thus, the hue of a rose may be used as a colorful accent in a light lily — or the shadows of a tulip may become the petal of a pansy, or the light throat of a petunia may become the petals of a small end flower.

Always bring something from your center bouquet out into

the scroll or other type of border. Thus the hue of a flower may be repeated as the vein of a scroll, or in the colorful accents in tips of the scroll. Or the varied shades of your leaves may be used as the body of your scroll.

One point I would like to stress particularly is a request that you do not change the outside border line that I give you on the pattern. This is the line on which you should turn your burlap to finish your rug, and when you hook beyond it, you are very apt to spoil the proportion of the design. So many times there are two or three inches of burlap beyond these lines. Some ruggers will hook as far as possible and thus get a bigger rug, but they utterly ruin the proportion of the whole design when they do so. There are a few of my older designs, especially antiques, where I copied the same proportion as was in the original rug, which might possibly be extended an inch — but not beyond that!

Now there is much more that I could write about the planning of your rug. However, if you wish to go beyond these general points, I would refer you to my Correspondence Course on Color, which is based on the Munsell System, and which is referred to at the end of this book.

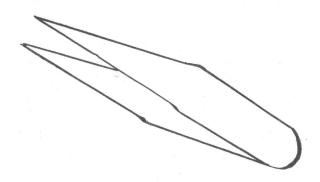

No. 440   GAINSBOROUGH

If you analyze the scroll of #440 Gainsborough (60 x 60) you will see it is a series of single scrolls. But it is my observation that it is the prettiest when the colors are used in a manner to give a continuous effect. Therefore a monochromatic treatment in which dark and light values are carried consistently through the entire scroll — or analogous hues which will flow together, and develop what we often refer to as a "painted" scroll — will give it continuity.

In the one illustrated, varied neutral gray materials in a variety of textures were used for the body, highlighting it slightly with a grayish-white, and veining it with soft reds and greens from the floral center. A mere suggestion of color was pulled into some of the knobby extremities. The reds were accented a bit more in the peacock eye border.

The reds were then intensified in the roses and the white was brought to a full highlight in the white tulip in the center.

Notice the red and green accents at the base of the white tulip — the repetition of reds in the veining of many of the leaves and in some of the ferns which gives them a reddish cast.

The whole development is a fine example of unity!

This is the design which brought me First Prize in design from the National League of American Pen Women, in Washington, D.C., in 1946.

No. 384   OLD COLONIAL

In a design of this type, (#384 Old Colonial, 75 x 100), where there is so much detail, simplify your color plan.

Dark and contrasting backgrounds have the tendency to make this rug appear smaller. A gradual transition from a medium dark edge to a lighter center will make it seem larger — or if there is only a slight difference in the background areas in light or medium values, it will appear larger still. Thus, your background is a very important factor!

If you choose a more or less monochromatic harmony it will solve your color problems and be very restful. Or, for a little more interest, swing into duller and soft shades of neighboring hues.

You will note that each cluster of flowers in the outer border is different. Carry something from each cluster into the next one, so that the eye easily follows.

Two tweeds which are similar, like a brown one with a blue pattern in it, and a blue one with a brown pattern, may be used for the large outer scroll — one as a filler for some of the scrolls in each group — the other as its outline or accented knob. Then reverse and use the other one as the filler in the others, with the first one as the outline and accent.

Don't dramatize these scrolls. The same materials may be repeated in the chubby inner scroll, but make the cropping leaves in similar or analogous hues.

No. 441   ROMANTIQUE

The manner in which a scroll is developed, and the choice of background beneath it, may result in a wide variety of color harmonies.

Here in #441 Romantique (34 x 60) notice how the scrolls blend from a soft jade green along the under side of each curl into an aqua upper side, or — in the case of the knobby ends — into chartreuse outer edges and knobs, accenting through the chartreuse highlights, the yellow-greens of the leaves within. Yet there is still a good balance between the soft jade shadows and the lighter blue-green leaves in the center.

Dramatic interest is given by the white 'mums against an extremely dark navy background.

We often refer to this development, where one hue is brushed into another through similar values of the two hues, as a "painted" scroll. It may be done also by "brushing" or fingering your colors together in the leafy curls, by starting off with one hue at the base, flaring it out lengthwise into a second hue and finally in the same manner into a third. Of course the sequence should be as they appear on the color wheel. Thus, the corner section of this scroll might blend from a purplish shadowed base into medium blues and thence out into lighter blue tips. The next section might blend from deep blue shadows into medium purples and thence into lighter lavender tips or knobs — while the third central section might repeat the first section, but possibly in lighter values of each.

No. 441   ROMANTIQUE (*a pair*)

It is always interesting to compare the same design worked out in two entirely different ways, as in this pair of Romantiques (#441, 34 x 60).

In one, note that the values of the outer background and the scroll are so nearly alike that they sink away into each other, forming a soft and subtle frame for the flowers within. Only a line of softly contrasting color saves the contour of the scroll from the outer background. The scroll is developed in a simple and quiet manner, with no contrast of shadow and highlight, throwing all the spot light to the floral center and corners. While the roses dominate the color plan, they are pleasingly supported by the secondary hues of tulip and mums.

In the other one, dark background accentuates the high lights of the knobs in the scroll — while the inner medium light background makes them appear wispy. The attention now is drawn to the realistically shaded roses in corners and center.

A sharp contrast between dark and light background in this design has always been popular. However, a medium dark inner background is intriguing too, for it permits the floral detail to subtly sink away into the surrounding area.

This design is pleasing too, when a soft subtle color is used for the inner background with the scrolls of neutral grays veined with a flower hue. In this case, keep the floral center more or less monochromatic, and use white flowers with colorful accents for interest.

No. 451   Chloris

Scrolls — and flowers too — need not necessarily be colorful! A restful and pleasing effect is obtained when color is used only to give accent and emphasis to neutrals.

Thus, in the rug illustrated, #451 Chloris (30 x 46) the feathery scrolls have been heavily veined in color, shading from rich purplish-reds at the dark knobby ends of the scroll — flanked on both sides with lighter values — and ending in mauve pinks at the lightest extremities. The body of the scrolls is blended from dark gray shadows flared out into the curls of the scrolls with varied grayish-whites fingered back into their darker values.

The large realistic rose and tulips repeat the feeling of the white scroll. Varied delicate grays are used for its greater area, with pure white only for highlights. Color is repeated from the scroll for its shadowy accents, or for delicate tinges in the white petals.

Whatever your color plan for this design, exaggerate the veins by flanking them on both sides with lighter values than those in the mid-rib, and drop the darker values soon after branching off into the side veins.

You can also give these scrolls a sculptured effect by using a slightly darker shade on the lower side of each vein to that used on the upper side. Or, you may use several values of one hue in each curl, shading gradually from a dark inner curve to a light outer curve.

In balancing color, there must also be a balance of dark and light values of colors. A rug is always much more interesting when there is a good balance between these two extremes.

Thus, in #414 Ayer Antique (40 x 85) you will notice how the dark values, or shadows, in the scroll are a pleasing contrast to the light ones, or highlights.

Notice, too, how the light values are fingered up into the dark values in the broad part of the scroll which makes it "turn over" — and how the dark values have been used along the outer curve shading off into highlighted knobs. A subtle touch is given near the center side where the light outer curve shades into a dark value at the tip and makes the extremity sink away into the background.

The same balance of extreme light and dark is carried into the center, where the very dark shades are massed in certain leaves, and the extreme light values show up in a few of the flowers. But naturally, there must always be that intermediate area of middle values leading up to both extremes.

The contrast of dark and light values is not limited to a single hue. You can safely use two hues flowing from the dark values of one into the light values of a neighboring hue. Thus the dark brown in a scroll may flow into light soft gold highlights — or dark greens may also flow into the same gold highlights.

No. 477   GAY NINETIES

The boldness of the floral wreath in #477 Gay Nineties (36 x 61½) dominates this design — the scroll border becoming of secondary importance. Its development must necessarily be in a "me too" manner, of a hue which binds it to either the floral or leaf colors in the wreath. Thus, you will notice how it is nicely linked, in subtle manner, to both the yellow-greens and blue-greens of the leaf detail, and its veining reflects the hue of the main flowers.

Notice too, how the green edges of the yellowish-white lilies save them from being lost against the rather light background.

Imagination is shown by the bluish leaves in the four curves of the wreath, which make a pleasing contrast to the others of yellow-green.

The background shows the uneven effect that we try to get, in dyeing materials for this purpose, which provides a delightful fluctuation — not enough to be "too busy" — but just enough to give it a distinctive interest.

Although the scrolls are grouped in small units, one should keep a feeling of continuity in the scroll as a whole, by flowing its colors, or values, together, so that there are no sharp or abrupt breaks in the color development. Thus, in this rug, you will notice that in some of the units the scrolls are rather dull and are blended of rather close values of one general hue, while in other groups they are blended in both yellow-greens and blue-greens — and some of them shade out into considerably lighter values at their tips — lending continuity to the border as a whole.

No. 496   WARE LEGACY (*a pair*)

The one-way rug has its place too. In a bedroom, #496 Ware Legacy (33 x 66) may be used before a chest of drawers.

Study this pair of designs, one with its scroll and floral detail in dominant hues against a simple background — the other, with its floral detail in apparently extremely soft coloring against a striking contrast in outer and inner background.

Keep a feeling of relationship between the leaves in the corners and the scroll. Treat both in similar coloring to give continuity to the border.

This border may be developed in a monochromatic manner, with the darkest values of one hue appearing in the corner detail and the base of the corner leaves, and gradually blending to light, or very light scrolls at center sides and ends.

Analogous colors — providing you use them in both leaf and scroll — will bind these details together. If the leaves are strikingly different from the scroll, either in value or hue, they may have a tendency to stand alone.

In the one with the light background, bronzy-greens flow into bronze and soft golds and back into bronzy-greens in the center scrolls, the golds reflecting the roses in the center.

Study the delightful imaginative development of the scrolls in the one with the two toned background, indicated by shadows and highlights. They gradually grow lighter toward center sides and ends.

I don't know why anyone should hesitate to make a room sized rug. After all, it is only like the accumulation of several smaller rugs. When the area of hooking is concentrated in one room sized rug it becomes of much more value. Any rug that requires a year or two to create, especially if well done with artistic taste, will naturally demand a good price. Usually one is loathe to sell such a rug when it is completed. Therefore you will seldom find them in the market for sale.

To me, hooking a rug of this size is like putting your time in the bank. Some day that time will turn to cash and may have accumulated "interest" besides. In the meantime you and all the family have enjoyed it.

#447 Dolly Varden (9′ x 12′) makes a priceless rug and serves as a spotlight of interest or a conversational piece for any room.

Here, in this illustration, the coloring has been kept quite simple but lovely, the main hues repeated again and again to give unity to the entire rug. Yet it is full of interest.

Notice the subtle change of backgrounds from the darkest value outside of the scroll border, changing to a lighter value in the intermediate area, and again into a third lighter tone beneath the floral detail.

Notice the pleasing complementary contrast of mahogany and turquoise blues — the latter scattered throughout the detail and accented in the bow knots on the baskets, but the former dominating in the color scheme as a whole.

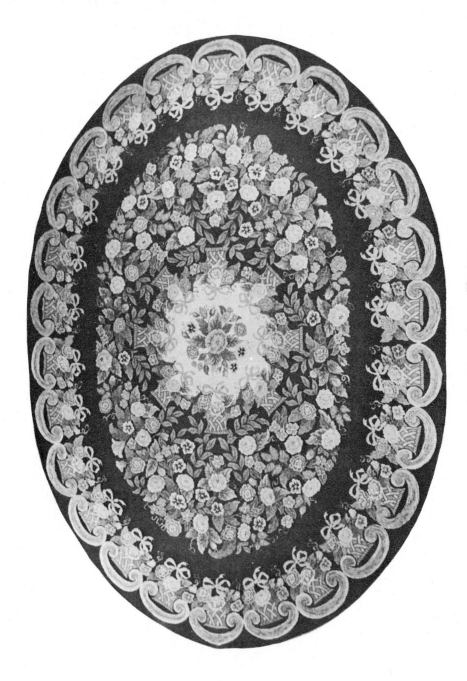

No. 447   DOLLY VARDEN

It is always intensely interesting to see what a different effect one gets through the choice of backgrounds.

Thus here again is #447 Dolly Varden (9′ x 12′) on an extremely dark background. It was a "raisin" shade — a sort of extremely dark reddish brown.

In this one, turquoise blue spot-dyed material was used for the scrolls — repeated in the ribbons — and scattered through the rest of the floral detail in which peach, soft yellows, and delicate lavenders dominated.

In a design like this, where repeating the baskets forms a border, it is best to develop the flowers in the same way in each basket. You may avoid monotony by varying the values of the hues of one flower with the same flower in the next basket. Thus, a peach or yellow rose may be a little lighter or darker than the same one in the next basket — but in a border like this you must not lose the feeling of continuity.

The same is true of the ribbons — while each bowknot may fluctuate and be a little lighter or darker in the different parts of the ribbon — they must never be darkened or lightened to the extent that they become spotty — or that they interrupt the feeling of oneness in the border.

Likewise, where the floral detail has been massed around the circular group of baskets, plan well — and repeat the hues you are using so that they are spread about in an even fashion. One should not look sharp or bright, or extremely light or dark in relationship to those around it.

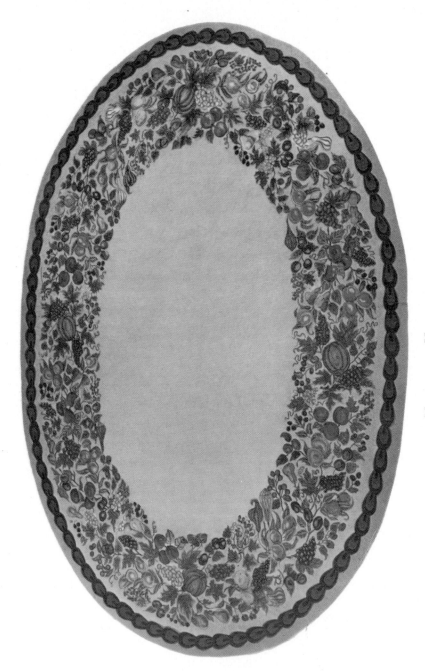

#444 Harvest (which you may have in either 8′ x 10′ or 9′ x 12′) makes a most distinctive dining room rug, which you may bind closely to your room by repeating its colors in draperies, walls and china.

For whatever their hues and no matter how realistically the fruit and berries are drawn, imagination in color, and in the manner of its development, will make it much more artistic than limiting yourself to reality.

For a peach does not have to be peach color, it may shade off from warm golden-browns to brownish-creams, if that color is important in your room. Grapes do not have to be purple, or red, or green — they may be a soft dull blue with exaggerated highlights of bluish-white.

Go to your museums and study tapestries as well as rugs. You will not find too many hues in one tapestry or rug, but you will find the hues used in many values and from their grayest to their most brilliant shades, and the colors may only be suggestive of realism.

In a design like this one, where the detail may be both large and small, use your brightest hues in the smaller areas such as the berries, and tone down the large details like melons, for instance, which may be soft grayed greens.

The peacock eye border permits a change to another background at the edge of the rug, if desired. Note the subtle change under the detail, growing gradually lighter at the center.

No. 139   MILLER SCROLL

This rug, #139 Miller Scroll (81 x 111) was my first original design in a room size. I made it years ago when I heard from a Mrs. Miller who wanted one with a wide border and "lots of flowers." But when it was finished she was afraid of its detail, and so she never made the rug which I had named for her. But countless others have — and love it!

I like the way this rugger has solved her problem of changing backgrounds by following the general contour of the inside of the scrolls so that the entire scroll lies upon the outer background.

Material is sometimes a problem in a large rug like this. If you will resort to the dye pot you will know no limitations. Any number of materials of a similar hue like a lot of varied dark browns could go into a pot bringing them into a little closer relationship through a dark brown bath. Likewise, materials of other colors may be turned to one general hue for an outer background.

Herringbones, tweeds, checks, colorless plaids and nondescript materials will take on glamor, via spot-dyeing, and provide a beautiful painted scroll.

Then for the light background, try taking the dye out of your materials — either by boiling in sudsy water, or through Cushing's Dye Remover, and see what delightful light backgrounds you will get for a light center like this.

A lovely one of my recollection was made from seventeen different grays from which color had been removed, resulting in palest pinky-white, bluish-white, lavender-white, and grayish-white. They were all mottled together and gave the loveliest opalescent effect to the background imaginable!

The use of white — or almost white — especially when repeated over and over again in small areas — is exemplified in the illustration of #490 Silver Dollar Scroll (54 x 88). It adds to the artistry of any good color plan.

The overlapping silver dollars which form a narrow border at the edge of this design have given the pattern its name. They are often made of neutral grays shading from oxford to silver white at the edges, as in the rug illustrated. Notice how the same series of grays are used for the small repeating scrolls around the floral center, and again — in the center — they form the lilies. Now if you were to examine the lilies closely you would find that their greater area is of subtly delicate grays, and only a small patchy highlight of the pure white is used at the center of the petals. Yet the general effect is a white lily, nevertheless. It's delightful!

Golden browns dominate the rug — in their richer shades in the large leafy scrolls in the outer border — repeated in an extremely dark value and weak intensity in the outer background — and again in a medium dull shade in the inner background.

There is also a nice repetition of bronzy-greens from the leaves within the large leafy scroll, the secondary leafy border within, and the leaf detail of the floral bouquet.

Even the wide variation of browns running into apricot and cream in the zinnias, petunias, phlox and cosmos, adds to the feeling of repetition within this rug.

No. 339   VICTORIAN SQUARE

There are many designs in square dimensions, and #339 Victorian Square (84 x 84) is an outstanding example of the mid-Victorian era. It was inspired by a rug in the Metropolitan Museum of Art.

The rug illustrated is on my living room floor at Rose Cottage, and is always greatly admired. Its outer background is a warm chocolate brown. The subtle interest in the inner background is a delicate honeycomb effect of three slightly different beigey-cream materials, the light to form the outlines, the dark to fill them, and the medium for the surrounding area. The darkest of the three shadows the area beneath the floral center.

The flowers (it's full of padulas) are an all-color harmony. Mulberry-rose dominates and all the other hues are subordinate to it, with contrasting blue-green and yellow-green leaves.

But to me the most interesting factor in this rug is the development of the scrolls. They are heavily veined in deep blue-greens which are repeated in one of the knobs in every other scroll, while in the knobs of the alternating scrolls are shades of lighter blue-green. The body of the scroll is filled with a taupey tan material which was spot-dyed with large splashes of soft green and grayed rose, but not enough to entirely cover the material. It was hooked in at random, so that each scroll took on a slightly different cast from the next one.

No. 532   DUKE OF MARLBOROUGH

All sorts of browns, from a medium dark chocolate brown blending out into a light brownish-cream were used for the scrolls in the rug illustrated — #532 Duke of Marlborough (34 x 60). It is veined in the purple and rose shades of the parrot tulip and roses of the center. The knobs of the scroll turn into a light soft blue-green, a reflection from some of the green leaves.

The background is an extremely dark brown — a nice tie-up to the golden brown chrysanthemums in the center.

This rug was made as a companion for a Gainsborough, in which the same dark brown background was used but with a blue-green scroll. The general hues in the flowers were the same in both rugs, but since the Gainsborough had the dominating position in the room (before the fireplace) and its scroll was more dramatic, we deliberately planned to make this rug play second fiddle to the other.

Notice the daintiness and lightness given to the white cosmos, by pinching the background closely to the center of the blossoms. You must cut fine to do it — but it pays.

It is always a great pleasure each year when finished rugs arrive for the annual exhibits to see how they will fit with the few furnishings shown with them. Last year a "Duke" arrived with a subdued mauve scroll with a pink and mauve floral center, that was just perfect with a pair of old fashioned carved walnut chairs upholstered with mauve velvet.

No. 497   LAVENDER AND OLD LACE (*a pair*)

There is another type of design which is neither scroll, floral, geometric nor oriental. Yet it has the curving line of scrolls, the conventionalized flower, the geometric detail, and — the broken backgrounds and odd shaped areas of the oriental.

#497 Lavender and Old Lace (26 x 63) contains them all. Its color combinations are unlimited. The difference in the pair illustrated shows how fascinating it may be to follow your own fanciful way in shading its intriguing detail.

Its name comes from the "lace" which scallops the border that encircles the center oval and forms the end panels.

In the left one only two hues were used, but in a variety of values and shades from deep wine to shell pink, contrasted with blue greens to aqua. The center detail is delicate rose and neutral grays and white, surrounded by soft blue green scrolls lying upon an opalescent background. In the two end panels, blue-green scrolls lie upon a deep dull mauve background. In the area surrounding the oval center and panel ends, the scrolls are mauve on an aqua background. A deep wine provides dark contrast under the whitish lace and for the dark outside background.

In the right one, dark browns, and greens, form most of the background areas, with scrolls of brown to cream, and lace of creamy-white. In the smaller detail, deep burgundy and medium rich rose provide color contrast.

No. 507   QUEEN'S DESIRE

When there is a great variety of flowers in a bouquet center, a mono-chromatic harmony will solve many of your color problems.

In the rug illustrated — #507 Queen's Desire (46 x 80) — all of the flowers were developed in the same hue, ranging from the deepest reds in the carnations to the delicate pinky veins of the white lilies. Blue-greens dominate in the leaves, thus repeating some of the wide variety of blue-greens used in the shading of the scrolls. (Since it is not always possible to reproduce the exact colors of a rug through the Kodachromes, my description of this rug is nearer to its true colors than the photograph.)

Because the two main hues used in this rug are complementary, it is nec-essary to gray the blue-greens and the pinks where they meet to form a pinky tip to the scroll. After the transition is made from one hue to the other, you can then shade out to a stronger pink. The scrolls are veined with the deeper shades of the rose-reds, but where the blue-greens lighten in the curling tips, the veins fade out into most delicate pinks.

Since this rug was made for a dramatic spot of interest in a room, a black outer background was used. The inner background was white spot-dyed in the most delicate tints of the varied pinks, blue-greens and the merest sugges-tion of yellow, so that they gave a slightly opalescent effect when hooked.

Sometimes when you obliterate part of my pattern you affect the propor-tion of my design. However, in this particular pattern, I planned it so you may omit the ribbon if desired.

A design like #541 Dowry Needlepoint (36½ x 62⅜) should have a definite needlepoint effect when finished. Therefore choose the soft colorings usually found in needlepoint patterns.

This design is authentic. It is from a choice antique, which I was permitted to copy. You'll love it!

The one illustrated was hooked very much like the instructions contained in the Dye Dabbler issued on this pattern, and quite like the original rug. Its blackish-green background in each block dramatizes the floral picture. The medium greenish-gray background in the border extends in between the squares — and the small detail at the intersection of the blocks should be of colors which will MELT into the background.

The narrow frame to each block is a spot-dyed material that changes and fluctuates, thus softening its outline. The same material was used for a narrow border within the blackish-green edge of the rug, thus binding edge to center.

The four different pictures are reversed on opposite ends. Thus, you have a chance to repeat your colors again and bind the pictures together.

The flowers were reddish grape, rose, pinky-browns, soft blues, corny yellows, blue-greens and bronzy greens.

Whatever hues you choose, use them again and again in the various blocks, even though it be only as a small accent in the center of a flower, or a shadowed throat of a blossom, so that the eye follows through the entire detail.

No. 472   Treasured Shawl

The scroll of #472 Treasured Shawl (30 x 48) may be gradually shaded from dark to light values of any one hue, or filled with mixtured materials — and paisley is one of the best.

This scroll has no vein, and in this illustration its outline is a medium deep Robin's Egg blue, spot-dyed so that it fluctuates from dark to light and forms a delightfully broken line of color against the outer background of black and the inner one of ivory. Three different paisleys were used in the scroll, one of which had considerable white and turquoise blue that gave the leafy detail individuality.

The center roses were keyed to the paisley reds, but in slightly lighter and softer shades. The canterbury bells repeated the Robin's Egg blues from the border, and I "married" the reds and blues, through dyeing, for the petunias. When you "marry" two widely separated hues (on the color wheel) like red and blue you get a good companion for both. Thus the hues of the roses and canterbury bells produced a soft shade of purple. The lilies at each end struck a delicate contrasting note of an extremely light soft maize.

I have seen this scroll shaded from medium golden browns that blend into delicate apricot against a dark brown outer and a brownish-cream inner background.

The floral center was almost monochromatic, with all the flowers brownish-golds to peach, all of which proves there is never just ONE way to do ANY pattern.

A TRIBUTE TO MY TEACHERS

Words seem inadequate to convey my feeling toward my teachers. My association with them has produced within me a depth of feeling far beyond that formed through the usual transactions of the business world. They are not just "an account" to me. They are very personal. Our dealings have tied many knots of friendship, not only between us — but by bringing them together — between each other.

Here I would pay my tribute to their enthusiasm for their work — their artistry in the development of my designs — their perseverance in bringing out the talents of their pupils — and their inspiration to all those with whom they come in contact.

Who are my teachers? I cannot attempt to name them — for the group grows each day — not by leaps and bounds — but slowly and surely, for that is the way I want it. Many of them are women of means, who are teaching for the pure joy of the craft — some of them have studiously prepared themselves for a more secure future — or found a way of earning a living when they faced tragic experiences. Thus my teachers come from all walks of life, and reside in 32 states. Some of those who became well known and loved in their communities have passed on, yet their names have become well known to all ruggers. Their influence — through their artistry — lives on. Perhaps by the time you read this book — for I do hope it will be of interest over a long period of time — new ones will have already become well known.

Addresses set down here would never be right. Many of them travel, bringing a new creative hobby to those with whom they come in contact. Therefore there would perhaps be no time when the list could ever be complete and correct.

You are naturally interested most in knowing those nearest to you, and a card of inquiry will bring their names and addresses.

What are the requirements for becoming a teacher? There

is no rigid rule. Many of my teachers are naturally craftminded. Hooking was an easy subject for them to master and teach. Some of them have had art training — some have painted — some have a natural flair for color — and some were proficient pupils, who having made a number of very good rugs, are passing on to others the lessons they have learned.

Since all teachers had to meet similar problems when starting new classes, I issued a pamphlet entitled "Training for Teachers." It is a requirement that all new teachers have this information, so that they may follow a general plan, and work, more or less, in unison. It is available to only those who have actually started classes — but not to pupils, or to those who think they might become a teacher later.

You can become a proficient teacher only as you have the actual experience of hooking. Even an artist will find that color, through the medium of wools, cannot be applied as oils or water colors. You must know what is hookable — how to develop details in a design, or apply accent and highlight, and be able to convey your ideas to another, so that they can put them into practice.

Imagination is a great help. This will often develop with teaching. Seeing rugs from start to finish will help to visualize what is going to happen when colors are hooked together. This will increase ideas. I like to think of ideas as flowing from a constant fountain, upon which you draw as necessary for each new problem. A teacher does not have to know all the answers in advance. As need arises, answers will be found.

The personality of a teacher is very important. Tact, with encouragement to those who are not — and possibly will never be good hookers — will help much more than hard and fast rules. For even though a teacher knows that a pupil might never produce an extremely good rug, she should not lose sight of other benefits she may be giving that pupil — and often such a one will eventually surprise her. A good teacher will not be too critical,

No. 436   Roseada

There is a certain feeling of freedom to the loose floral arrangement of #436 Roseada (48 x 78).

The rug illustrated hangs in the Studio at Rose Cottage and attracts much attention.

Repetition in the lily near the center is a "marriage" of the yellow highlights (in its center) from the brown tulips, and the brownish-reds (in colorful accents at the petals' edges) from the roses. The sweet peas reflect the center purple tulip and are balanced at the extreme opposite end by forget-me-nots (or padulas) of the purplish-blues of some of the petunias.

Dull and grayish-purples from the inner tulip are suggested in the turn-over tips of the tulip leaves. The largest leaves are heavily veined with the grayed hues of the varied flowers.

All of the leaf greens (and there are 27 of them) are used in developing the three tiered shell border — the darkest values in the outer row shading to a medium value at the edge — the medium dark values in the middle row shading to light values at the edge — and the medium values in the inner row shading out to extremely light values along the inside edge.

The inner background is interesting because two very close values of a light grayed beige have been mottled together in a very fine honeycomb effect, to become as one! Their separate identities are apparent only on close inspection. Most subtle!

but see and comment on the good, until pupils have set their stride. Then, a little tighter rein will help them to improve or reach a higher standard.

But most of all, a good teacher will know the subject of color. Aside from good design, it is the most important part of a rug. There are many teachers who can teach the technique of hooking, but a good one will also know color.

Some knowledge of interior decorating is of great advantage, because, after all, these rugs must fit into homes. This is another reason why the understanding of color is so very important. Sure, many women can hook — hook beautifully — and turn out a rug in excellent technique, but its color must be good to fit into its proper place and add grace to a room.

Realizing this, I sought a universal language in color, to make its use and discussion more understandable when teachers gathered together. I found this in the Munsell system of color, in which there could be an identification of any hue, by its value and its intensity — a system which is used throughout the world. So I developed a correspondence course based on this system, in which we use a set of 362 color cards. Not that color can be confined to a few hundred values and intensities of hues, but through these few, we could learn to understand the law and order of color, and describe it more accurately when talking and writing. It is especially slanted toward the use of color in hooked rugs. The course calls for the development of certain color plans as applied to a definite type of hooked rug design, which I can review and report upon. It develops an ability to visualize the effect one may achieve when certain colors are applied to a given area. Constructive criticism of the application of color to hooked rugs is provided during and at the end of the course.

In my effort to help my teachers, I have drawn them together as often as possible in recent years to offer them a chance to put into practice new ideas to carry back to their classes.

In the summer of 1949, six of my teachers accompanied me

to South Carolina where we held a week's session at Blythe Shoals (the summer camp of the Parker District School). It was really intended for the residents of that district, but we had registrants from eight surrounding states, and it was therefore made available to others. It was amazing to see the progress in their work at the end of just one year. So these have become annual events, which are of great benefit to the teachers themselves, for it brings them together for discussion of mutual interest.

There have been many other similar occasions, the most recent of which was in the early part of 1951. It came about through making my sister Kaddy my Western distributor in order to give quicker service to teachers on the west coast. She has a Studio in Sherman Oaks, California, and during my visit there she cooperated with me in an effort to give the same personal assistance to the western teachers as I have given to those in the East. We held several two day conferences and work shop sessions in her Studio in which the teachers carried out new ideas to give to their pupils.

There is no stress brought to bear upon these teachers to use only my designs, yet from choice, the majority have become "exclusive" with my patterns. They say, "I like them better, I know how to interpret them, and I can do a better job for my pupils." Thus McGown teachers are becoming recognized throughout the country for their artistic work. Teachers have learned that their interests are mine, and that I leave no stone unturned to help them in their work.

How do they conduct their classes? In varied ways — often through local Women's Clubs, civic organizations, churches or neighborhood and small private groups. Of late years, many of them are teaching in State Adult or Vocational Training Schools. Their pupils are young and old — the healthy and the ill — those full of zest and those who are escaping boredom — those who have finished bringing up the family, and are finding a great void to be filled.

No. 87   BELMONT SCROLL

There is nothing more fascinating than developing graceful curves like those in #87 Belmont Scroll (36 x 68) for they offer an unlimited variety of interpretations in color.

This one has been most artistically "painted" with two complementaries, mahogany and peacock. Note how the large mahogany scroll in diagonal corners gradually changes to peacock. The artistry comes from mingling the two hues in proper proportion and of the right values, where they meet. The transition must be gradual and subtle. Thus you will notice that the peacock is first introduced as only a suggestive note at the edge of one curl. But in each succeeding curl it appears more frequently until it entirely takes over, with the light mahogany now showing only as a vein. Notice how light values are used at the end of the curls lying against the dark outer background, while bright intensities of the peacock help to lift the curls of the scrolls from the inner background.

The wild roses repeat the light values of mahogany, but are intensified to a mahogany pink, shading into creamy centers. The leaves reflect the peacock scrolls with its darker values blended into their greens.

There is a definite relationship between the extremely dark outer and the medium inner background, but you will note the browns are a weaker intensity, thus proving a good foil for the richer shades of mahogany.

These teachers do not always conduct their classes in their own home town or city, but oftentimes travel many miles to their pupils. Some go two or three hundred miles, and stay for several days or a week at a time.

Naturally, in a small group or in a private lesson, a teacher has much more time for individual instruction. Therefore, pupils will progress much faster in this type of class. In the Adult School classes, where there may be as many as thirty to fifty pupils, progress depends upon the ability of the pupil to grasp the instruction of the teacher from the blackboard. The teacher propounds upon certain principles which may be applied to the individual's rug, regardless of the colors being used, and refers to her sketches in showing how to blend or "finger" colors together, or where to place shadows and highlights in flower or leaf.

Teaching is a very broadening experience. I have seen extremely quiet and meek personalities fairly bloom under the experience of having something worthwhile to give to others. It creates self confidence. When a new teacher starts — especially if her pupils are novices, it is as though she knew ALL, but she must, of course, keep constantly alert to gain new ideas and thus keep ahead of her pupils.

Often as I look through my list I am thrilled with the thought of how many women have found in this craft a new way of life. I recall the joy in one teacher's voice as she confided that she had always been a home body, with little time or thought for aught else but her family's needs. Then one day she found that her responsibilities were over. The hobby which she had managed to tie in with her home life turned to a way of earning her living. (For many of my teachers will be found in small villages.) It took her out into other homes and into the lives of other people. She loved people, and she found each personality of interest. Her pupils loved her too — they were always surprising her with some little evidence of their thoughtfulness. "Oh, I LOVE what I am doing — every day is a thrill!" she would say.

Teaching is a challenge, and if accepted, one will grow through every new experience. To be faced with planning the colors of a rug to tie in with those in a room becomes a fascinating problem. In solving it one gains new ideas in color, and ingenious ways of combining color to achieve artistic effects.

It is true that teaching is not easy, for one never quite drops the thought of class and pupil. A teacher will carry home the image of a rug not quite right, and the problem of how to correct it. A color may be lacking and must be dyed without formula, and only the benefit of experiment. A teacher's mind will churn with how a scroll may be developed, or even personal problems like that of how to deal with selfish pupils who demand all her time. Her phone will ring constantly with demands of "I need another pound of that dark brown background, and will you dye it for me before the next lesson?" — or meek inquiries of "I've forgotten whether you said to use my fourth lightest shade for the highlight of my rose, and I *do* want to have it finished before next class." No — teaching hooked rugs is not easy —but it *is* most fulfilling! For the day comes when the rugs are finished and brought in for inspection— and the "Ohs" and "Ahs" of other pupils are some of a teacher's compensations.

But perhaps the greatest compensation to a teacher is what this craft does for the pupil.

They are not only learning how to make a hooked rug. Their lessons are a mental uplift and even have a therapeutic value as well.

Regardless of the fact that pupils may seem impersonal when they come into a class, they are not that way long. Not that pupils always unburden their mind of their cares and problems — (though some do) — but gradually you learn something about each one from others, and you begin to realize what hooking is doing for them. This day spent in class with others is a "magic carpet" carrying them away from rough reality — they come in perhaps still worrying about the thing which is on their mind — but they go home thrilled with the "blooming of a new tulip" or the fascinating development of a lovely scroll. "Oh you don't know what this day has done for me," they say.

I have seen a pupil who in her first classes had to jump up three or four times an hour to smoke a cigarette, become so enthused over her work that only one sufficed at the lunch hour. I know of one pupil who comes to class, takes a lesson on a rug, and goes home to give it over again to a loved one to keep them away from alcoholics.

I have known of pupils who appeared regularly at classes, and never by word or sound would one know they were suffering from an incurable disease.

I know of mental cases where a hooked rug has been the one step between a normal life and one in an institution.

But I would not have you think that a hooked rug class is only for the mentally and physically ill. No indeed, it is for those who enjoy the companionship of kindred spirits and those who gain inspiration from the work of others. It is for those who get a thrill from their own accomplishment which will turn their hours into something worth while, with some evidence of how they are spent. It is for those who love their homes — the center point of interest for all family life.

The young are never too young to learn to hook — teach them early. Young girls make hooked rugs for their Hope Chests. Young matrons find a way to bring beautiful rugs to their floors which they could not afford to buy. Mothers find recreation in creating new rugs, not only for their own floors, but as gifts to sons and daughters. Grandmothers dote on making them for two and three generations back. It is a craft enjoyed by all, because it is creative.

The thrill of the year for teachers and pupils alike comes each May, when for many years I have sponsored a Teachers' Exhibit in the Horticultural Hall, in Worcester, Massachusetts, lasting three days.

My teachers send me examples of their work of the year, usually some unusual interpretations of color, or the development of some of the newer designs (issued each Fall) which will be an inspiration to others. Here three hundred or more rugs ranging from the small to full room-size are displayed.

Distance does not prevent California teachers, as well as those from the Middle West, North and South from joining us in the East. They find help and inspiration for another year in the ideas which are brought out in the Teachers' Day Conference which precedes these exhibits, after which the exhibit is opened to the public for the following three days.

These exhibits attract thousands of visitors to Worcester. It is not unusual to see busses roll in filled with eager ruggers from Wisconsin, South Carolina and many other states.

Allen Eaton, in his book "Handicrafts of New England" says: "These Exhibits are attended by persons from all parts of New England and from many other states. The various processes of dyeing and hooking are demonstrated. Prepared materials, with instructions as to how they may be used with some of the patterns, are available at reasonable cost. There is a general interchange of ideas and experiences among hookers and teachers. This is probably the most important annual gathering of rug makers in our country."

In this year of 1951, they gathered their work together in their first National Western Exhibit, which was held in the Hollywood Masonic Temple Auditorium on February 22, 23 and 24. Emphasis was given to the work of the western teachers, although all others contributed to it too. For the first time those on the West Coast were privileged to visit and enjoy an Exhibit like those which have brought so much pleasure to so many ruggers during the National Exhibits in Worcester, Massachusetts.

I would also pay tribute to the thousands of pupils who contribute their artistry to these Exhibits, and my gratitude for the illustrations herein.

CARE OF HOOKED RUGS

When your rug is completed, it should have a good steam pressing. The steam takes care of any unevenness in your rug and will give it a finished look. If a small size, turn it upside down on your ironing board, but if large, it is better to use a larger area — if necessary, the floor. Since the rug will become quite damp do not place it on a varnished surface, or floor. Protect either one with a heavy covering of papers and blanket. Press with a wet thick turkish towel and a good hot iron. Then turn your rug, cover with damp cloth and press lightly on the right side. Let it remain perfectly flat upon the floor until thoroughly dry.

Before placing your rug in the chosen spot, it is also advisable to sew a marker on its back with your name and address, the year it was made, and any other desired information. Since the rugs you are making will last long enough to be heirlooms, those who will inherit them will appreciate the information. If they fall into other hands the markers may add to their value. You will not always be around to proudly say "I made that!" We have learned through attempts to identify the age of antique rugs that some such identification would have been priceless in establishing their values.

When moving a rug from one place to another — don't drag it, roll it up and carry it.

When transporting your rugs, never fold them — always roll them, over a small tight roll of newspapers, and always with the right side of the rug on the outside of the roll. The reason for this is that as you roll, the loops spread and give, and there is no added strain to the burlap foundation. I know you'll say, "But that will bring a light delicate background on the outside where it might get soiled." True, but you can protect that with a cloth cover.

Never, never shake a hooked rug!

You may use a vacuum cleaner on your rugs if they have been hooked by the technique I recommend, for then all ends have been brought to the top of the rug, and they cannot be pulled out even by suction. But from my own actual experience I found that the type of vacuum cleaner that has a beating motion as well as suction is too harsh for a hand hooked rug.

From my own experience, too, I believe that home shampooing is superior to commercial dry cleaning. It does not have to be done too frequently either. My rugs at Rose Cottage get extremely hard wear, yet some of them will go for three to five years before they need shampooing.

I advise the same care in cleansing them that you would use with any prized possession. I have cringed when I heard some women say they put their rugs in a washing machine. I would as soon put a baby through such a bath.

First clean well with your vacuum, and that means both sides of the rug. Then lay the rug over a kitchen table (it's easier on your back) preparatory for cleaning. Personally I like Jalma (a fine powder recommended for dainty underwear and usually found in department stores) but I have also used, in moderation, Ivory Snow and Lux. Make a suds with fairly hot water. Dip a small brush (a 5¢ vegetable brush does nicely) in the water and go over an eighteen inch square to make a lather. Wring out a cloth in clean warm water and go over the same space, picking up and absorbing the soap and lather. Change both suds and rinse waters frequently as necessary. Don't get the rug any wetter than necessary. After all, if you have used the vacuum on your rugs frequently, the soil lies upon the surface of your rug. Lay the rug where it can remain flat for 24 hours until dry. If it is on a porch where the sun and wind can get at it, so much the better. But in such a case, spread newspapers first, to absorb some of the dampness and aid drying.

They always look so appreciative of this care!

Have you ever thought how long it would take to replace your rugs? Only those who have hooked rugs can appreciate the loss which might occur through fire.

Adequate insurance will off-set in part some of the tragedy and serve as some recompense for the time you spent in making them.

Regular fire insurance is affected by the depreciation that comes with time. Thus, the amount you collect may be reduced with the years. Because of this and the time element of replacement, I suggest you consider a Fine Arts policy. Under this, the valuation is not affected by depreciation, and since we know these rugs grow more valuable with the years, this point is worth considering.

List of Back Issues of LETTER SERVICE
Other Than Those Subjects Treated Herein

(All available at 15¢ each)

List of Back Issues of LETTER SERVICE
Other Than Those Subjects Treated Herein
(All available at 15¢ each)

List of Back Issues of LETTER SERVICE
Other Than Those Subjects Treated Herein

(All available at 15¢ each)

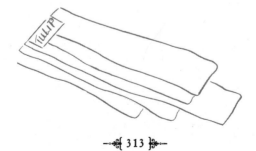

LIST OF PATTERNS
TREATED BY THE DYE DABBLER†

	Pattern Number	Size	Subject	No. of Dye Dabbler
Amish	528	32⅝ x 51		37
Arcadia	422	30 x 57	Scroll	16
Arcadia	422	30 x 57	Floral Cen.	17
At Long Last	476	15¼ x 45		23
Backgrounds				6
*Basket Weave	332	37 x 55		55
Breath of Spring	487	23¼ x 38		15
Calla Lily Wreath	63	32 x 60	Border	53
Calla Lily Wreath	63	32 x 60	Floral Cen.	54
Cascabel Stair Runner	514	27″ wide		27
Chilcott Leaves	191	36 x 68½		39
*Cluster Checkerboard	190	32 x 56		36
Color Remover				19
Criss Cross	538	28⅞ x 46⅛		50
*Cross & Roses	SD2	36 x 63		45
Cushing New All Fibre Dyes				34
Dowry Needlepoint	541	36½ x 62⅜		49
*Fascination	526	24½ x 39½		42
*Filigree	567	27 x 44⅛		57
Fireside Fancy	483	35½ x 44		10
First & Second Fiddle	484	28 x 46	Scroll Border	11
First & Second Fiddle	484	28 x 46	Floral Cen.	12
Gay Nineties	477	36 x 61½	Floral Cen.	22
Gay Nineties	477	36 x 61½	Scroll Border	24
Gifford Aubusson	238	34 x 58¾		48
Gift of Dreams	469	32½ x 66	Floral Cen.	1
Gift of Dreams	469	32½ x 66	Leaf & Sc. B.	2
Glad Hand	516	28 x 42½		46
Gloxinia Scroll	480	36 x 62½ Oval	Scroll Border	7
Gloxinia Scroll	480	36 x 62½	Floral Cen.	8
Hand Bag	4	10 x 10		9
Harmony	537	30 x 48¾		47
Heart's Desire	517	20 x 40		33

†Back issues of "Dye Dabbler" available at 25¢ each.

LIST OF PATTERNS
TREATED BY THE DYE DABBLER† *(Continued)*

	Pattern Number	Size	Subject	No. of Dye Dabbler
Hill's Leaves	338	30½ x 52		30
Hunter Wiscasset	253	37 x 55		32
It's a Cinch	524	24½ x 37½		38
Lavender & Old Lace	497	26 x 63		43
Lush	511	24 x 35		44
Maple Rhythm	489	30 x 59		18
Morning Glory Bunny	174	30 x 40¼		56
Nantucket Scrollings	{ 74	25½ x 52		5
or	{ 96	36 x 45		
*New England Twist	60	24½ x 45¾		61
Ollivia	398	48 x 88	Scroll	20
Ollivia	398	48 x 88	Floral Cen.	21
Peace	525	32¾ x 49½		41
Perfume Box	492	29 x 54		31
Pillow Top	1	14 x 14		9
Quaker	564	36 x 64		58
Scalloped Scroll	129	38 x 66		52
Season's Promise	500	28 x 46	Scroll	26
Season's Promise	500	28 x 46	Floral Cen.	25
Seven Sisters	503	33 x 55	Scroll	28
Seven Sisters	503	33 x 55	Floral Cen.	29
Staffordshire Oval	539	60 x 101		
		Oval	Floral Cen.	59
Staffordshire Oval	539	60 x 101	Border	60
*Strawberry Patch	533	27 x 43¾		40
Tinker Scroll	171	29½ x 61		35
Treasured Shawl	472	30 x 48		4
Twirly Whirly	468	20 x 30		14
Wind-blown Flowers (Anemones)	471	14 x 32		3
*Winter Bloom	485	30 x 50½		13
Woodland Sprite	563	32 x 58		62
Young Man's Fancy	494	24½ x 41		51

*May be ordered in other sizes.
†Back issues of "Dye Dabbler" available at 25¢ each.

LIST OF OTHER PUBLICATIONS

PAMPHLETS

DYE PAMPHLET — beginner's dye instructions .... $ .35

THE RAINBOW IN RAGS — complete instructions for dyeing —
a "must" for creating beautiful hooked rugs 1.00

THE GIST OF GEOMETRICS — with 24 illustrations and suggestions for colors in 17 different designs 1.00

OBJECTIVES IN ORIENTALS — with instructions for each little
motif and border in 9 different Oriental designs 2.00

PICK & CHOOSE and PICK & CHOOSE, TOO — two descriptive
lists of my hooked rug designs (but not illustrated) 1.00

COLOR COURSE — a correspondence course on COLOR, based
on the Munsell system — including a set of 362 color swatches,
and formulas to obtain each. Especially slanted toward the practical application of color to hooked rugs, including constructive criticism on two pieces of hooking 50.00

TRAINING FOR TEACHERS — fundamentals and principles of
teaching, and ways of conducting classes — available only to my
group of teachers 5.00

✦   ✦   ✦

My book, "THE DREAMS BENEATH DESIGN"— a story of the
historical background of the old original and early American
designs of hooked rugs, with many interesting stories concerning
the rugs and those who made them. A delightful and authentic
bit of Americana. A charming gift book — artistically designed
and profusely illustrated — recommended by the American
Library Association 2.00

NOTES

NOTES

NOTES

NOTES